AMERICA'S NATIONAL PARKS

GREAT SMOKY MOUNTAINS
NATIONAL PARK

AMY GRAHAM

MyReportLinks.com Books
an imprint of

Enslow Publishers, Inc.
Box 398, 40 Industrial Road
Berkeley Heights, NJ 07922
USA

MyReportLinks.com Books, an imprint of Enslow Publishers, Inc. MyReportLinks®
is a registered trademark of Enslow Publishers, Inc.

Library of Congress Cataloging-in-Publication Data

Graham, Amy.
 Great Smoky Mountains National Park : adventure, explore, discover / Amy Graham.
    p. cm. — (America's national parks)
 "A MyReportLinks.com book."
 Includes bibliographical references and index.
 ISBN-13: 978-1-59845-093-4 (hardcover)
 ISBN-10: 1-59845-093-X (hardcover)
 1. Great Smoky Mountains National Park (N.C. and Tenn.)—Juvenile literature. I. Title. II.
Series.

 F443.G7G723 2008
 976.8'89—dc22

                                    2007013456

Printed in the United States of America

10 9 8 7 6 5 4 3 2 1

To Our Readers:
Through the purchase of this book, you and your library gain access to the Report Links that specifically back up
this book.
The Publisher will provide access to the Report Links that back up this book and will keep these Report Links up
to date on **www.myreportlinks.com** for five years from the book's first publication date.
We have done our best to make sure all Internet addresses in this book were active and appropriate when
we went to press. However, the author and the Publisher have no control over, and assume no liability for, the
material available on those Internet sites or on other Web sites they may link to.
The usage of the MyReportLinks.com Books Web site is subject to the terms and conditions stated on the Usage
Policy Statement on **www.myreportlinks.com**.
A password may be required to access the Report Links that back up this book. The password is found on the
bottom of page 4 of this book.
Any comments or suggestions can be sent by e-mail to comments@myreportlinks.com or to the address on the
back cover.

♻ Enslow Publishers, Inc., is committed to printing our books on recycled paper. The paper in every book
contains 10% to 30% post-consumer waste (PCW). The cover board on the outside of each book contains 100%
PCW. Our goal is to do our part to help young people and the environment too!

Photo Credits: APN Media, LLC, p. 11; Appalachian Trail Conservancy, p. 56; AP Photo/*The Daily Times,* Tom
Sherlin, p. 95; cherokee-nc.com, p. 30; Discover Life in America, p. 98; discoverbluegrass.com, p. 114; *Doubletoe
Times,* p. 115; Environmental Protection Agency, p. 83; Friends of Great Smoky Mountains National Park, p. 96;
gatlinburg.com, p. 111; Great Smoky Mountains Institute at Tremont, p. 97; HistoryNet.com, p. 33; Hunter
Library Special Collections, Western Carolina University & the Mountain Heritage Center, p. 45; istockphoto.com,
pp. 1 (Stacey Putman), 6 (Cades Cove) & 60 (Jill Lang), 7 (cabin) & 48–49 (EyeMark), 8–9 (Darrell Young), 15
(Joseph Abbott), 38–39 (Eileen Hart), 54–55 (Dave Hughes), 100–101 (Beverley Vycital); Knoxville-TN.com,
p. 19; LeConte Lodge, p. 110; Library of Congress, p. 26; MyReportLinks.com Books, p. 4; National Park
Foundation, p. 61; 1 (Stacey Putman), National Park Service/Enslow Publishers, Inc., p. 5; National Park Service,
pp. 1, 6 (Eastern redbud trees) & 18, 22, 42, 53, 66–67; National Parks Conservation Association, p. 116; PBS,
pp. 47, 86; Shutterstock.com, pp. 3 (Smokies with clouds) & 102–103 (Matej Krajcovic), 6 (river otter) & 90–91
(IRC), 6–7 (top banner) & 108–109 (Jerry Whaley), 7 (salamander) & 78 (BZ Photos), 8–9 (computer), 12 (Ryhor
Zasinets), 20 (Nikita Tiunov), 24–25 (Darryl Vest), 42–43 (camera), 58–59 (Tony Wear), 62–63 (Tony Campbell),
71 (Susan Kehoe), 75 (Bruce MacQueen), 80–81 (FloridaStock—haze photo), 80–81 (laptop), 85 (Jan Gottwald),
94 (Thomas & Amelia Takacs); The Sierra Club, p. 69; *Smithsonian,* p. 82; The Smithsonian National Museum of
Natural History, p. 72; Tennessee Wildlife Resources Agency, p. 77; tnvacation.com, p. 106; The University of
North Carolina, p. 17; visitnc.com, p. 14; Wheeling Jesuit University/Center for Educational Technologies, p. 64;
The WOOLAROC Museum, pp. 34–35; Woodland Park Zoo, p. 92.

Cover Photo: © istockphoto.com/ Stacey Putman (inset photo); National Park Service (background)

CONTENTS

MyReportLinks.com Books
Great Books, Great Links, Great for Research!

The Internet sites featured in this book can save you hours of research time. These Internet sites—we call them **"Report Links"**—are constantly changing, but we keep them up to date on our Web site.

When you see this "Approved Web Site" logo, you will know that we are directing you to a great Internet site that will help you with your research.

Give it a try! Type http://www.myreportlinks.com into your browser, click on the series title and enter the password, then click on the book title, and scroll down to the Report Links listed for this book.

The Report Links will bring you to great source documents, photographs, and illustrations. MyReportLinks.com Books save you time, feature Report Links that are kept up to date, and make report writing easier than ever! A complete listing of the Report Links can be found on pages 118–119 at the back of the book.

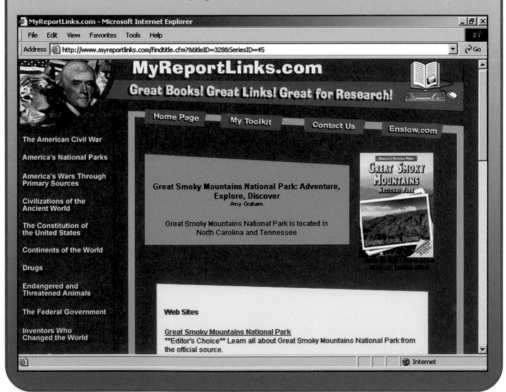

Please see "To Our Readers" on the copyright page for important information about this book, the MyReportLinks.com Web site, and the Report Links that back up this book.

Please enter SMP1527 if asked for a password.

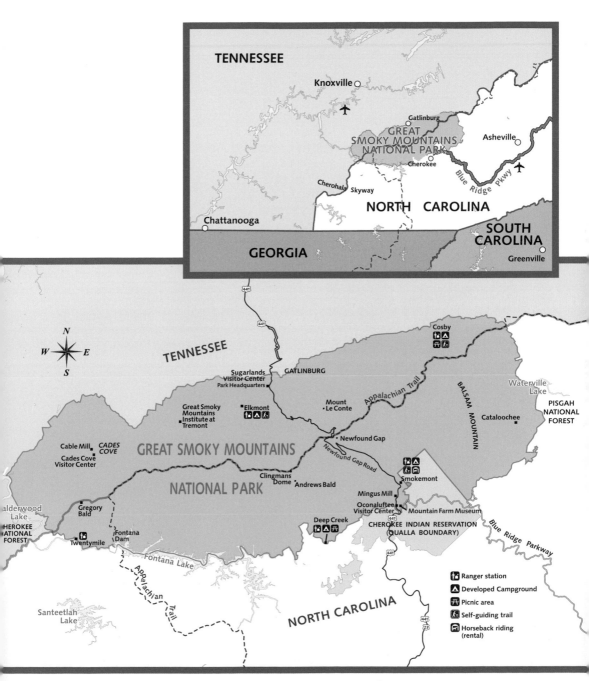

▲ Great Smoky Mountains National Park straddles the border of North Carolina and Tennessee. The Appalachian Trail runs through the park.

Great Smoky Mountains National Park is located in the southeastern United States. It straddles the border of North Carolina and Tennessee.

The Great Smoky Mountains are part of the Blue Ridge Mountains, a southern branch of the Appalachian Mountains. The Appalachian Mountains run from Georgia to Maine.

The park is 521,086 acres. It extends roughly 65 miles (105 kilometers) from east to west and 25 miles (40 kilometers) from north to south.

More than 9 million people visit the park each year, making it the most visited national park in the United States.

Clingmans Dome is the park's highest mountain peak at 6,643 feet (2,025 meters). It is the third-highest mountain east of the Mississippi River.

The Appalachian Trail runs through the Great Smoky Mountains on its way from Georgia to Maine. Clingmans Dome is the highest peak on the entire trail.

The park has twenty summits higher than six thousand feet.

There are thirty-six miles of continuous mountain ridgeline over five thousand feet high.

The U.S. Congress authorized the formation of the park in 1926. Crews of the Civilian Conservation Corps (CCC) worked to get the park ready during the Great Depression. The park was officially established on June 15, 1934.

President Franklin D. Roosevelt dedicated the park at Newfound Gap in 1940.

In 1983, the park was designated a World Heritage Site in recognition of the many plants and animals that thrive here. The park was named an International Biosphere Reserve in 1988.

National Park Facts

The Great Smoky Mountains are the ancestral homeland of the Cherokee Indians.

There are one hundred species of trees in the park, more than in all of northern Europe.

In the early 1900s, timber companies logged two-thirds of the park. Even so, the park contains the largest tract of old-growth forest in the eastern United States.

Fifteen of the largest trees in the United States are located in the park.

The mountaintops receive an average of eighty-five inches of precipitation each year, making it a temperate rain forest.

There are roughly fifteen hundred black bears in Great Smoky Mountains National Park (GSMNP), or about two bears per square mile.

In 2001, elk were reintroduced into the park. The native elk population was hunted to extinction by 1750.

At least thirty different species of salamanders live in the Smokies, making the Smokies the "Salamander Capital of the World."

Unlike at other national parks, people do not pay a fee to enter Great Smoky Mountains National Park. This was a condition of a five-million-dollar grant from the Laura Spellman Rockefeller Memorial Fund, as directed by John D. Rockefeller, Jr.

The park has ten campgrounds, with more than one thousand campsites.

More than nine hundred miles of hiking trails crisscross through the park.

There are seventy-eight historic buildings still standing in the park, including log cabins, churches, schools, and mills.

Chapter 1

A view of the Great Smokies in summer.

A Trip to the Great Smoky Mountains

Anna and her parents were beginning their spring vacation to Great Smoky Mountains National Park. It was April, and Anna had a week off from school. As the family made its way to the park from the airport in Knoxville, Tennessee, they stopped to consult a map. They had no trouble locating the national park: it stood out as a large patch of green, free from highways and towns. It straddled the border of Tennessee and North Carolina. Anna had not realized the park's area was so large (more than half a million acres, or eight hundred square miles).

Spring had already begun in Tennessee. Unlike at home in Vermont, there were already leaves on the trees and the weather was pleasantly warm. Anna began to look forward to the fun of exploring somewhere new.

The Smokies are part of the Blue Ridge Mountains, in the Appalachian mountain range. "The Appalachian mountain range runs up the entire East Coast, all the way from Georgia to Maine," Anna's mom explained. "But the mountains here are a little different because the glaciers never came down this far. Our northern mountains were scoured by a thick layer of ice, but the Smokies never were. You'll see just how rugged and tall they are compared to our gentle mountains back home."

→SUGARLANDS AND LAUREL FALLS

After staying overnight at a hotel in Gatlinburg, Tennessee, the family's first stop the next morning was the Sugarlands Visitor Center in the park. The center seemed more like a small museum, with exhibits of plants and animals that live in the park. Anna and her parents watched a short film about the Smokies and the park's history.

A ranger asked about their plans for their visit, and Anna's father asked him about waterfalls. He had heard the Smokies had many cascades. The ranger explained that spring is a great time of year to see waterfalls, since the rushing streams are full of rainwater. He told them about a nearby trail to Laurel Falls. Did they want to see it? He showed them the trailhead on a map. It was an easy one- to two-hour hike along a paved path. Anna agreed this sounded like the perfect place to eat the picnic lunch they had packed.

A few minutes later, Anna and her parents were making their way along the path. The sun was out, and it promised to be another warm day. Chickadees flitted through the woods. Anna thought the little birds' calls sounded friendly and

Great Smoky Mountains National Park | Oh, Ranger! - Microsoft Internet Explorer

File   Edit   View   Favorites   Tools   Help

Address http://www.ohranger.com/smoky-mountains   Go   Links

HOME   PARKS   ACTIVITIES   NEWS & EVENTS   PLAN YOUR TRIP

Oh, Ranger!

For Answers To
All Your Questions™

Great Smoky Mountains National Park

In Depth

○ Great Smoky Mountains
   National Park
○ Activities & Programs
○ At Your Fingertips
○ Campgrounds in the Great
   Smokies
○ Camping at Great Smoky
○ Did You Know : Battles
○ Did You Know : Families
○ Did You Know :
   Photography
○ Did You Know : Smokies
○ Flora

Great Smoky Mountains National Park

Welcome to Great Smoky Mountains, comprised of ridge upon ridg
straddling the border between North Carolina and Tennessee. Th
renowned for its diversity of plant and animal life, the beauty of i
and the quality of its remnants of Southern Appalachian mountain
800 miles of trails, America's most visited national park is a hiker's

APPROVED WEB SITE

Done, b

Oh, Ranger!: Great Smoky Mountains National Park presents an informative overview of the park and details about its history, flora and fauna, and geology. Sights to see there and activities to do both in the park and in nearby Gatlinburg, Tennessee, are also covered.

cheerful. As one landed on a tree twig near her head, she held her breath and stood very still. The chickadee cocked its head to the side and gave her an inquisitive look. Anna couldn't help laughing at its expression. She regretted startling the bird, which flew away to rejoin the flock. She and her parents followed the path up through the oak and pine trees.

As the family reached the end of the trail, they could hear a waterfall. The trail rounded a corner, and there it was. A mountain stream burst out of the shrubs overhead. A wall of white water poured

Laurel Falls is one of the most popular destinations in the park. The falls are named after mountain laurel, an evergreen shrub that grows nearby.

down the side of a hill. It must have fallen fifty feet before it landed with a splash in a pool.

Anna made her way over boulders to the water's edge. Spray splashed up in her face. From the pool, the water fell once more, before the stream continued gently on its way down the hill. The rush of the water and beauty of the scene enchanted the girl.

CLINGMANS DOME

After their hike to the waterfall, Anna and her parents decided to drive up Newfound Gap Road. This road, also known as U.S. Route 441, is the only major route in the park. From Gatlinburg, it winds seventeen miles through the mountains up to Newfound Gap. A gap is a low point on a mountain ridge where it is easiest to cross.

Newfound Gap marks the border between Tennessee and North Carolina. After the road enters North Carolina, it twists and turns back down the mountains to the town of Cherokee. Anna quickly grew dizzy in the backseat as the car zigzagged around tight bends in the road. At one point, the road passed through a tunnel and looped back over on itself. To Anna's stomach, it felt like a roller-coaster ride, and she had to ask her mother to slow down. They pulled over at a turnout at the state line.

Anna was glad to stand on firm ground after the stomach-churning ride. A nearby monument

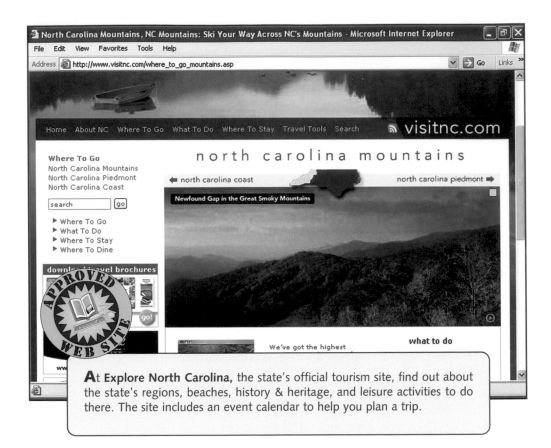

North Carolina Mountains, NC Mountains: Ski Your Way Across NC's Mountains - Microsoft Internet Explorer

File   Edit   View   Favorites   Tools   Help

Address http://www.visitnc.com/where_to_go_mountains.asp   Go   Links

Home   About NC   Where To Go   What To Do   Where To Stay   Travel Tools   Search   visitnc.com

north carolina mountains

Where To Go
North Carolina Mountains
North Carolina Piedmont
North Carolina Coast

⬅ north carolina coast   north carolina piedmont ➡

Newfound Gap in the Great Smoky Mountains

search   go

▶ Where To Go
▶ What To Do
▶ Where To Stay
▶ Where To Dine

download travel brochures

go!

We've got the highest   what to do

At **Explore North Carolina,** the state's official tourism site, find out about the state's regions, beaches, history & heritage, and leisure activities to do there. The site includes an event calendar to help you plan a trip.

commemorated the day in 1940 when President Franklin D. Roosevelt had dedicated the park. From here, they could see into North Carolina. A few minutes after they had climbed back into the car, they saw a sign for Clingmans Dome—the highest mountain in the park. Anna's mother took a winding side road to see the view. Miles later, she slowed the car to a stop in a large, paved parking lot. "This way to the observation tower," her father pointed out. They followed a steep, half-mile trail to the summit.

The forest here was quite different from down below in the valleys. It reminded Anna of the forests on the mountains at home in New England. The trees were almost all evergreen. Patches of snow still clung to the ground, and the mountain air felt cool and thin.

Then Anna began to notice dead trees on either side of the trail. Some were blown over, decomposing on the ground. The skeletons of others still stood. They creaked as they swayed in the wind. There

A view of the Great Smoky Mountains from the summit of Clingmans Dome, the highest mountain in the park at 6,643 feet.

were so many that it looked like a ghost forest. Anna asked her father what had killed off the trees. He explained that "a tiny insect, the balsam woolly adelgid, killed them. It sucks the sap from fir trees for food and damages the trees in the process. The insect is an exotic, invasive species—it did not live here originally, but now that it does, it is taking over and harming native plants. I read all about it at the visitor center."

Moments later, an observation tower came into view. Anna thought it looked like a giant toadstool. She followed her parents as they climbed up the spiral walkway. At the top of the stairs, Anna stood and gazed at the view. Now she could see what was so special about the Smoky Mountains. Mountain ridges stretched out across the land in each direction, as far as she could see. She felt awed by the sight. She snapped a few pictures with her camera to help her remember. No matter how hard she tried, she just could not capture the feeling she had. It was like being on top of the world!

THE MYSTERY OF THE MOUNTAIN BALDS

Anna sat on a rock and looked over the map with her parents. They were making plans for the next day. "We should take a hike to Andrews Bald. There's a trail from the parking lot. Why do you

CAROLINA ENVIRONMENTAL DIVERSITY EXPLORATIONS

ELEVATIONS AND FOREST TYPES · BY DIRK FRANKENBERG

SELECT A PAGE ▾ | START ▸

Elevations and forest types along the Blue Ridge Parkway

BY DIRK FRANKENBERG

This Carolina Environmental Diversity Explorations "virtual field trip" explores the great range of forest types found in North Carolina's Blue Ridge Mountains, which are as diverse as those found at lower elevations from North Carolina to Canada. You'll learn about chestnut oak forests, rich cove forests, northern hardwood forests, spruce-fir forests, and the strange "balds" of the mountains where no trees grow, and you'll learn about the environmental factors that create this incredible diversity.

START YOUR FIELD TRIP ▸

What are Carolina Environmental Diversity Explorations?

Carolina Environmental Diversity Explorations are virtual field trips to areas characterized by both beautiful scenery and useful lessons about North Carolina's environment. Our state stretches from the Appalachian mountains to the sea. Along the way you can find rocks formed when the earth was only half as old as it is now, climate zones equivale...

Carolina Environmental Diversity Explorations: Elevations and Forest Types

This site provides a "virtual field trip" spotlighting the forests found in the area of the Great Smoky Mountains, including "mountain balds," a type of mountain meadow. The presentation covers the area's biology and history, and a glossary defines scientific terms.

Access this Web site from http://www.myreportlinks.com

suppose it's called a bald?" Her father looked up from the guidebook he was reading. "A bald is a kind of mountain meadow. I just read something about balds." He frowned. He flipped back a few pages. "Here it is. Did you know there are dozens of heath and grassy balds in Great Smoky Mountains National Park?" he asked.

"No one is sure how the balds first began," her mother read over his shoulder. "Some experts believe that, long ago, wildfires burned these patches in the forest. The fire burned so hot that the flames spread underground. Even the tree roots burned, and the trees never grew back. Shrubs, such as mountain laurel and rhododendron, took

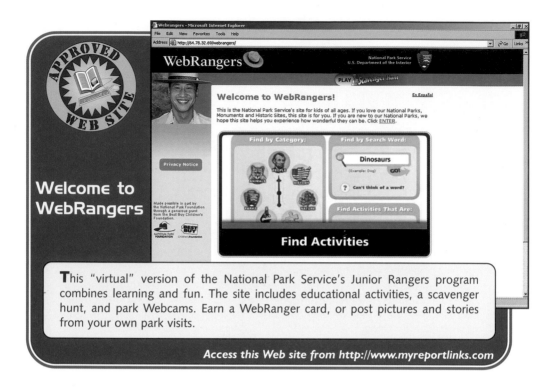

This "virtual" version of the National Park Service's Junior Rangers program combines learning and fun. The site includes educational activities, a scavenger hunt, and park Webcams. Earn a WebRanger card, or post pictures and stories from your own park visits.

Access this Web site from http://www.myreportlinks.com

over. They grow so thick and dense that no tree seeds can survive. Other balds are grassy. Settlers grazed their livestock there. In earlier times, herds of elk and bison browsed on the balds."

"Sounds interesting," said Anna. They made plans for a hike and a picnic. But the next day, they were disappointed to hear that it was snowing in the mountains. The road to Clingmans Dome was closed! It was hard to believe, since the weather in Gatlinburg was sunny and 55°F (about 13°C). Instead of exploring up high in the mountains, the family decided to go on a wildflower tour. A park ranger at the visitor center told them it was Spring Wildflower Pilgrimage Week in the

Smokies. Experts lead tours of people out every day to view the flowers.

⊜ SPRING WILDFLOWER PILGRIMAGE

Their tour guide pointed to a patch of white flowers, and Anna stooped to take a closer look at one. Six white petals surrounded a yellow center. It hung toward the ground, and she lifted it up with her hand. The guide said it was called a mayapple. Anna's mother waved her over. The forest floor was carpeted with tiny white flowers. "Fringed phacelia," said her father. "See the fringe along the edge of the flowers? It gives them a wispy look."

Wildflowers are one of the many delightful sights in the Great Smoky Mountains. Here, Knoxville-TN.com presents a gallery of dozens of wildflower species, along with descriptions of their distinctive qualities.

Access this Web site from http://www.myreportlinks.com

The yellow lady's slipper is just one of many wildflowers that can be found on a hike through the park. The flower's four thin petals surround its yellow pouch.

Anna stood and looked around. It was amazing how many flowers they had seen on their hike today. The air was cooler here than it was down below in Gatlinburg. Still, there was no sign of snow. From town, she had seen the mountain peaks covered in clouds. She was glad she had on her fleece jacket. At this elevation, the forest trees were still bare of leaves. Without the leaves to soak up the sunlight, the forest was bright. Once the leaves came out, the tree canopies would shade the forest floor. In the summer, shade-loving ferns would grow. But for now, the sun shone on the many flowers that grew on the forest floor.

⇨ THE LADY'S SLIPPER

Wildflowers bloomed everywhere. Anna's favorite so far was the yellow lady's slipper. She had been the first of the group to spot it. The delicate lady's slipper had looked out of place. Four thin, wavy, yellow petals stood around a yellow, slipperlike pouch.

The tour guide had explained how the lady's slipper gives off a spicy smell to attract insects. The flower needs an insect to pollinate it. Most flowers attract insects with tasty nectar. But a bee that flies into the pouch of a lady slipper is out of luck—there is no food there. In order to escape from the pouch, the bee must push its way through a tiny passage. As it does this, it leaves pollen from the other plants it has visited. The plant gets what it needs, but the bee must keep looking for food.[1]

Now the guide led them farther down the trail to a patch of green. They trudged through a carpet of last year's brown leaves. The leaves crunched beneath their boots. As Anna got closer, she could see the green leaves hid white, almost light pink, flowers. Each flower had three large petals in a whorl. The guide told them the name: white trillium.

On the way back to the car, their trail followed the banks of a stream. Anna could hear the water

▼ *The white trillium's flowers change to a darker pink as it ages.*

gurgle as it rushed over the mossy rocks. Thick rosebay rhododendron bushes grew up on either side of the path. They were tall, even taller than her father. In one spot, the shrubs leaned in to form a tunnel over their heads. Their large evergreen leaves shone glossy in the sun. Anna admired them out loud. The guide told them how, in June, the bushes were covered with large white and pink flowers. That night, as Anna fell asleep, she marveled at all the flowers she had seen on their tour.

Chapter 2

Grist mills like this one were built in the park in the 1800s.

Cherokee, Mountain Men, and Timber Companies

The Smokies are among the oldest mountains in the world. To better understand how they were formed, we have to look back to between three hundred and two hundred million years ago, when the continents of North America and Africa collided.

The earth's crust lies beneath the oceans and the continents. It is made up of large, continent-size pieces called tectonic plates. These plates move very slowly, at a rate of a few inches a year. Where the plates collided, the rock buckled and folded. Older layers of rock were forced up over younger rock. The displaced rock piled up, forming the Appalachian Mountain range.[1]

The Smokies are part of the Blue Ridge Mountains, which are in turn a small part of the Appalachian Mountains. These southern Appalachians, taller than their northern counterparts, were never topped by glaciers as the northern mountains were.[2] Instead, water and weather have played a large role in form-

Try to imagine the Smokies as they were twelve thousand years ago. A herd of huge, elephant-like animals called mastodons graze in a grassy valley. One lifts its trunk and trumpets a warning. The herd breaks into a run and the ground trembles. Mastodons once lived all across North America.

A hungry band of hunters lies in wait, spears at the ready in their hands. The Paleo-Indians—early American people originally from Asia—were hunters, always on the move. They followed their food source: herds of wild animals like the mastodon. These early people also foraged for wild plants to eat. They left little behind, so we do not know much else about how they lived.

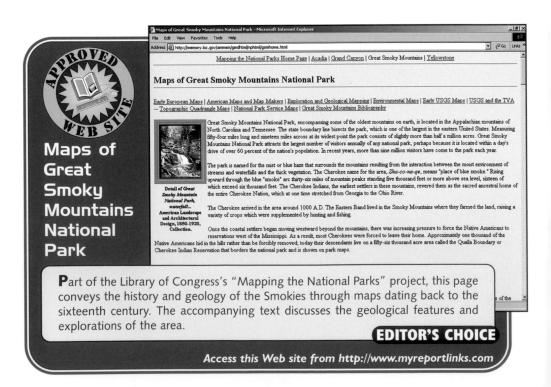

APPROVED WEB SITE

Maps of Great Smoky Mountains National Park

Part of the Library of Congress's "Mapping the National Parks" project, this page conveys the history and geology of the Smokies through maps dating back to the sixteenth century. The accompanying text discusses the geological features and explorations of the area.

EDITOR'S CHOICE

Access this Web site from http://www.myreportlinks.com

Now let's jump ahead to 1000 B.C., or three thousand years ago. People's way of life had greatly changed by this time. They lived in villages in the river valleys, hunted elk, deer, and bison with bows and arrows, and ate fish that they caught in nets. They grew crops of the "three sisters": corn, beans, and squash, carved gourds to make birdhouses, and hung them in the fields. The birds ate the insects that fed on the crops. People buried their dead in dirt mounds, much as we use cemeteries today. Trade routes linked them with other communities.

HEARTLAND OF THE CHEROKEE

By the time Christopher Columbus set foot in the New World, the Cherokee Indians lived in the Smoky Mountains. Long ago, they had been part of the Iroquois tribe of New York. They broke away from the main tribe and, over the years, slowly moved south. They settled in the southern Appalachians at least five hundred years ago.[4]

The Cherokee were a powerful tribe. Their land spread all the way from Kentucky to Georgia. Their heartland was in the Smoky Mountains. The Cherokee believed their land was at the center of the world. They believed that they were the chief people.[5] The Cherokee tell a story about the first man and woman. Their names were Kanati and Selu. Like Adam and Eve, these first people lived in a beautiful land. They lived in the Great Smoky Mountains.

The Cherokee built their houses out of logs and mud. They covered the roof with tree bark, with a hole for a chimney. The hole let in light, too, for there were no windows in their homes. At the center of the village was a large council house. The council house had seven sides and a domed roof. This is where they met for festivals and religious ceremonies. Men gathered to smoke tobacco and discuss politics. Here, too, Cherokee warriors planned raids on neighboring tribes. A warrior was a high-ranking person in Cherokee society.

IN SEARCH OF GOLD IN THE NEW WORLD

In the year 1540, sailing ships set anchor off the coast of Florida. Hernando de Soto of Spain led his men to shore. He believed there were great riches in the New World. De Soto and his men set out on an overland trek. They met the Cherokee on their travels through the Southeast.

De Soto did not find any gold, but he did open the door for the Spanish to come to the New World. They soon built forts along the coast of Florida. The Spanish traded with American Indians, including the Cherokee. The Cherokee brought them pelts of deer, beaver, and bison. They swapped the fur pelts for seeds, livestock, tools, and weapons. In Europe, people had over-hunted fur animals until there were few left.

People used the fur to make coats, hats, and other warm clothing.

Sadly, American Indians also caught new and devastating diseases from the Europeans. In 1750, an outbreak of smallpox swept through the Cherokee Nation. It spread like wildfire. When it was over, half of the Cherokee people had died.[6]

⇒ CULTURE CLASH

It had been Cherokee tradition to hunt only what they needed. Now they killed many more animals so that they could trade. They were eager to get their hands on weapons, and hoped to gain the upper hand in their battles with enemy tribes. As the numbers of deer, bison, and elk shrank, the Cherokee had to search farther. This brought them onto enemy lands. The British, Spanish, and French settlers had killed many bison and elk, and so did the Cherokee. The herds shrank, until one day they were gone.

The settlers still had their cows and pigs to depend upon for a meat source. But the Cherokee had depended on the wild animals for their meat and leather. Their way of life was changed. The settlers and the Cherokee often did not see eye to eye. For instance, settlers had no problem killing a deer on Cherokee land. The Cherokee believed wild animals did not belong to anyone. But if a hungry Cherokee killed a pig on a settler's land, it

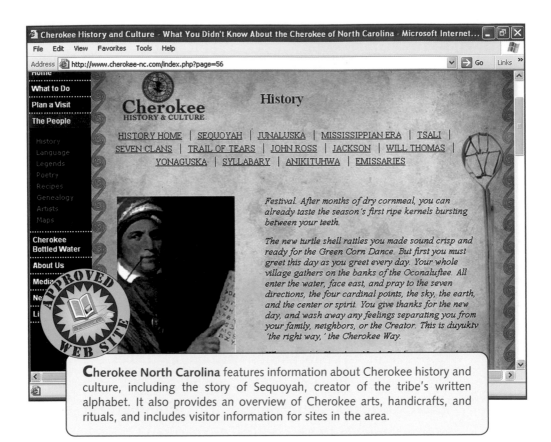

Cherokee History and Culture - What You Didn't Know About the Cherokee of North Carolina - Microsoft Internet...

File   Edit   View   Favorites   Tools   Help

Address http://www.cherokee-nc.com/index.php?page=56   Go   Links

Home
What to Do
Plan a Visit
The People
  History
  Language
  Legends
  Poetry
  Recipes
  Genealogy
  Artists
  Maps
Cherokee
Bottled Water
About Us
Media
Ne
Li

Cherokee
HISTORY & CULTURE

History

HISTORY HOME | SEQUOYAH | JUNALUSKA | MISSISSIPPIAN ERA | TSALI |
SEVEN CLANS | TRAIL OF TEARS | JOHN ROSS | JACKSON | WILL THOMAS |
YONAGUSKA | SYLLABARY | ANIKITUHWA | EMISSARIES

Festival. After months of dry cornmeal, you can already taste the season's first ripe kernels bursting between your teeth.

The new turtle shell rattles you made sound crisp and ready for the Green Corn Dance. But first you must greet this day as you greet every day. Your whole village gathers on the banks of the Oconaluftee. All enter the water, face east, and pray to the seven directions, the four cardinal points, the sky, the earth, and the center or spirit. You give thanks for the new day, and wash away any feelings separating you from your family, neighbors, or the Creator. This is duyuktv 'the right way,' the Cherokee Way.

Cherokee North Carolina features information about Cherokee history and culture, including the story of Sequoyah, creator of the tribe's written alphabet. It also provides an overview of Cherokee arts, handicrafts, and rituals, and includes visitor information for sites in the area.

was grounds for death. This did not seem very fair to the Cherokee.[7]

→ THE AMERICAN REVOLUTION

In the eighteenth century, more people came to North America to escape the crowded cities of Europe. They spread across the East, looking for more land. American Indians grew worried. Would there be any land left in the future?

When the American colonists fought the Revolutionary War with the British, the Cherokee took a chance. They signed a treaty with the king of Britain.

If Britain won the war, King George would keep the colonists off Cherokee land. The Cherokee agreed to fight on the side of the British. But the gamble did not pay off; the British lost the war. American colonists felt the Cherokee should pay a price for siding with the enemy. They set fire to their homes and crops. The Cherokee fled to safety in the mountains.

→ SEQUOYAH'S TALKING LEAVES

The Cherokee did not have a written language. They told stories, sang songs, and danced. That is how they passed on knowledge to one another. Sequoyah was a Cherokee who worked with silver. Like other silversmiths, he signed his work. He learned to spell his name in English. This gave him an idea. Why not create a Cherokee alphabet? He decided he would try.

Sequoyah gave each sound in the Cherokee language a letter. When he was done, he had eighty-six letters. He taught his new alphabet to his young daughter Ah-yo-ka. He and Ah-yo-ka would play a game to demonstrate the alphabet to people. Sequoyah would have someone ask him a question. He would write the answer down on a piece of paper. Then he would call Ah-yo-ka in from outside. She would read the answer.[8]

Other Cherokee liked the idea of Sequoyah's "talking leaves." In 1821, the Cherokee made it the official written language of their nation. Within two years, nearly all Cherokees had learned to read and write. They soon began to publish a newspaper, the *Cherokee Phoenix*. They wrote down their laws. Like the Americans, they wrote a constitution to define their government. These were great steps forward. Yet the Cherokee Nation was growing weak. Disease and years of war had taken a toll. The Cherokee Nation faced a growing threat—the desire of the white settlers for more land.

INDIAN TERRITORY AND THE TRAIL OF TEARS

In 1830, Congress passed the Indian Removal Act. The government would take over the Cherokee's land. As a trade, they would give the Cherokee land in Oklahoma. It was not a very good deal for the Cherokee. But for some, it looked better than continuing to fight. President Andrew Jackson was a staunch supporter of the act. He was a soldier who had fought many Indian tribes in his day, and he was eager to free up land in the East.

The Supreme Court did not agree, and struck down the Indian Removal Act. The court said Congress had no right to make decisions for the Cherokee Nation. President Jackson was furious. He challenged the Supreme Court justices to uphold Congress's ruling.

To get around the issue, President Jackson persuaded a small group of Cherokee to sign the Treaty of New Echota. Under the treaty, the Cherokee gave up their land. The treaty was legal, even though it was against the will of Cherokee leaders and most of the Cherokee people. Army troops marched into Cherokee land and forced the Cherokee to leave their homes. They rounded up fifteen thousand men, women, and children and guarded them in forts. Conditions in the forts were very poor, and there was not enough food.

The soldiers forced the Cherokee to march at gunpoint. With heavy hearts, they trudged all the way to Oklahoma. It was a trip exceeding one thousand miles. More than four thousand Cherokee died of disease and hunger along the way. The

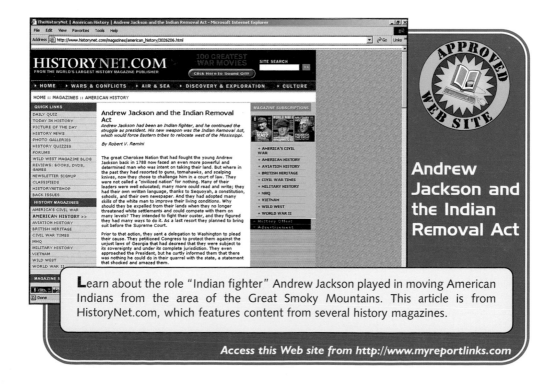

Learn about the role "Indian fighter" Andrew Jackson played in moving American Indians from the area of the Great Smoky Mountains. This article is from HistoryNet.com, which features content from several history magazines.

Access this Web site from http://www.myreportlinks.com

Artist Robert Lindeaux's famous painting of the Cherokee people on the Trail of Tears.

Cherokee call it Nunahi-duna-dlo-hilu-i. It means "the trail where they cried," best known as "the Trail of Tears."

Not all Cherokee went west to live in Indian Territory; some stayed behind. If they bought their own land, the government could not make them move. Nearly one thousand Cherokee refused to go west on the Trail of Tears. They hid from the soldiers and fled into the hills. They lived there, in fear for their lives, for many years.

In 1848, Congress agreed to recognize the Cherokee's rights if the state of North Carolina recognized them as permanent residents. In 1866, North Carolina formally recognized the Eastern Band of Cherokee. By 1924, tribal lands were finally placed in federal trust to ensure that they would forever remain in Cherokee possession.

Today, the Cherokee live on more than fifty-six thousand acres in North Carolina. Their land is the Qualla Boundary Reservation. The people who live here have found a balance between their traditions and life in modern-day America. Many speak and write in the Cherokee language.

⇒ AMERICANS SETTLE THE SMOKY MOUNTAINS

As long as the Smokies were part of Cherokee land, not many other Americans had tried to settle there.

For one, the rugged mountains were imposing. They were difficult to enter from North Carolina, so most settlers skirted around them.

Hardy settlers ventured into the Smokies. These pioneers had little money to their names. They went in search of land they could work and call their own. The settlers built rough log cabins in isolated coves, and hunted bear, deer, and wild turkey for meat. They raised pigs, feeding them on the chestnuts and acorns that fell from the trees each autumn. They chopped down trees and cleared stumps to make fields where they grew corn and wheat. These settlers lived hardscrabble lives, worked hard, and often went hungry.

⇒ CIVIL WAR IN THE SMOKIES

The mountain folk worked from dusk until dawn to make ends meet. That was not the case for all people in the South. Some wealthy Americans owned large farms called plantations. They grew crops of tobacco and cotton, and kept slaves to do the work. They thought of their slaves more as animals than people.

But in the northern states, a growing number of people thought it was wrong to keep slaves. People who spoke out against slavery were called abolitionists. They wanted to abolish, or put an end to, slavery. This would destroy the way of life in the South.

So eleven southern states broke away from the United States and formed the "Confederate States of America," or what Northerners called "the Confederacy." Americans had fought hard for their freedom in the Revolutionary War, and the Union (or the North) was not about to let the young nation fall apart. In 1861, the North and the South went to battle in the Civil War. Even though they lived in the South, many of the mountain folks sided with the North. They did not have much sympathy for the wealthy slave owners.[9]

It became dangerous to live in the Smokies. While no major battles were fought there, both Union and Confederate troops marched through the area. They showed little respect for private property. Soldiers broke into farms and houses and took whatever they pleased. Some Cherokee fought in the Civil War, too. They fought on the side of the South, for some wealthy Cherokee owned slaves as well.

After four years of bloodshed, the Union forces won the war against the Confederates. In 1863, President Abraham Lincoln issued the Emancipation Proclamation. It stated that every American has the right to be free. It outlawed slavery once and for all.

This log cabin, nestled in a cove in the Smokies, is typical of the dwellings that settlers built there before the Civil War.

➔ "TIMBER! LOOK OUT BELOW!"

As the twentieth century began, a great change came to the Smoky Mountains. Large timber companies bought up huge tracts of land. They had already cut the forests in the Northeast and West. Until now, they had passed over the forests of the South. The mountains were just too tall and too rugged. But thanks to a new kind of train with gears, they could lay railroad tracks through very steep mountains. Trains could get to those hard-to-reach trees.

The timber barons eyed the acres upon acres of huge trees growing in the southern Appalachians. Soon the woods rang out with the sound of axes and saws. The timber companies brought many jobs to the area. The jobs came at a time when it was hard to make a living on a farm.

For many of the rural mountain folks, it was the first time they had wage-paying jobs. They worked long days, and the work was dangerous. Many of the loggers were rough-living, single men who spent their pay at the pool hall each weekend on alcohol.[10] But family men worked in the woods, too. They brought their families to live in the logging boomtowns. There the children could attend school.[11]

Sadly, timber companies gave little thought to what they left behind. They did not think about what the forests would look like after they were done, or care about how their actions affected the wildlife that lived in these woods. They thought only about how much money they could make in profits.

The beautiful, ancient mountain forests were cleared of trees. Loggers put dynamite in the creeks to blow up any boulders. They rolled logs into the water and drove them downstream to the mill. In other places, trains carried logs to the mills. The trains gave off sparks that sometimes burned into wide-spreading fires.

With the forests cut down and burned over, the Smoky Mountains were far from a scenic wilderness in the 1920s. The view from Clingmans Dome was horrific. Tree roots no longer held the soil in place. Mud slid down the mountains, clogging the creeks. The once majestic Great Smoky Mountains were now an unsightly ruin.

Chapter

3

An autumn view taken from Newfound Gap, the lowest pass through the Smoky Mountains.

The Birth of Great Smoky Mountains National Park

The timber companies were always on the lookout for ways to make more money. They knew many people came to the Great Smoky Mountains to vacation and sightsee. They had already built railroads through the mountains to pull the logs out. Why not add a car to the end of the train for passengers? People might be willing to pay for a trip through the mountains.

They were right: people did like the idea. But their plan backfired, for many people did not like what they saw. The trains took them through the forests that had been heavily cut. The damage stood out in stark contrast to the beautiful, old-growth forests. People began to talk. How could they preserve the Smoky Mountains from further logging?

CONSERVATION MOVEMENT

In 1872, Yellowstone became the first national park in the country. Soon, there was a call for more national parks. It was really quite simple to create parks out West because the land there was publicly owned.

In 1893, the state of North Carolina urged Congress to establish a park in the Southeast. The government would have to buy the land. Farmers owned the fields that dotted the coves. Timber companies owned large swaths of woodland. A farmer who was struggling to get by might be persuaded to sell his land. But it was not so easy to get a timber company to sell, not at a reasonable price. During World War I, lumber was worth a great deal of money.

In 1923, the National Park Service agreed to form a park in the Appalachian Mountains. They toured many sites. The Great Smoky Mountains topped the list. The peaks were rugged and picturesque. The valleys were deep and fertile. There was a great variety of plant and animal life. Now they had to convince people that a park was a good idea.

SUPPORTERS AND OPPONENTS OF THE PARK

For years, Horace Kephart lived alone in a remote cabin in the Smoky Mountains. He had moved to the Smokies to write books about the way of life in the mountains. As part of his research, he met many local folk. He hunted bear with hound dogs and kept company with bootleggers.

Bootleggers secretly made their own whiskey, which was against the law. They brewed their "moonshine," as the whisky was called, from corn. They hid their equipment deep in the brush where the police would not find it. And, occasionally, they exchanged gunfire with the law. Kephart wrote about these people in his book, *Our Southern Highlanders.* The book was a hit. Many Americans read and enjoyed it.

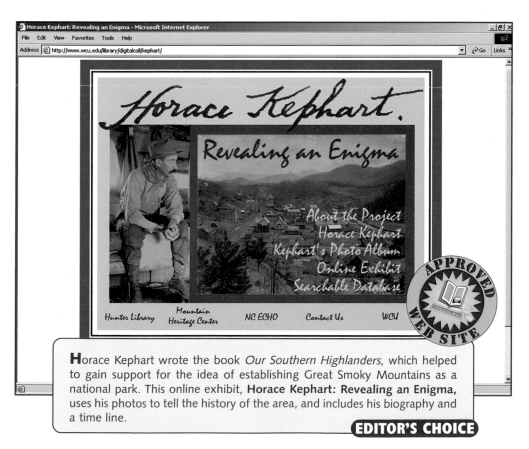

Horace Kephart wrote the book *Our Southern Highlanders*, which helped to gain support for the idea of establishing Great Smoky Mountains as a national park. This online exhibit, **Horace Kephart: Revealing an Enigma,** uses his photos to tell the history of the area, and includes his biography and a time line.

EDITOR'S CHOICE

Kephart had grown to love the splendor of the mountains. He did not like the destruction of the forests. He backed the idea of a national park in the Smokies, and used his gift with words to describe the beauty of the mountains he loved and why they should be saved.[1] His hard work, combined with the efforts of photographer George Masa, paid off. People in the area grew to support the idea of a park.

THE CAUSE WINS MORE SUPPORT

In Knoxville, Tennessee, a group of people joined the cause. They formed the Great Smoky Mountains Conservation Association. People in both Tennessee and North Carolina wanted to preserve the mountains. State and city governments raised money to help fund the park. School children saved pennies for the cause. A national park would bring much-needed jobs to the area.

The federal government spent $2 million on land for the park. Still, it was not enough. Thankfully, millionaire and philanthropist John D. Rockefeller, Jr., stepped in to help. He designated $5 million from the Laura Spellman Rockefeller Memorial Fund to the project. He had one requirement: admission to the park must always be free to the public.

Some people did not think the park was a good idea. At the top of the list of opponents were the

American Experience: The Rockefellers

A $5 million grant from the Laura Spellman Rockefeller Memorial Fund is the reason why there's no admission fee to the park. This Web site, companion to a PBS documentary, examines the Rockefeller family through essays, photographs, video interviews, and more.

Access this Web site from http://www.myreportlinks.com

timber companies. They would lose profits if they sold their land. Several of them went to court to argue their case.

Champion Fiber Company was at the heart of the controversy. It owned ninety thousand acres right in the center of the proposed park. The company produced paper from trees at their mills. Without its lands, there could be no park. Champion Fiber owned Mount LeConte and Clingmans Dome.

John W. Oliver was another opponent of the park. He was one of twelve hundred people who lived in the Smokies. His family had been some of the first people to settle in Cades Cove. His kin had

A photo of John Oliver's cabin. Oliver's family had been living in the area for one hundred years, and he was a vocal opponent of the park's formation.

been living off this land for the last one hundred years. Oliver did not think it was fair he should have to move. He felt a tie to the land that no money could replace, so he fought the government with all his might.

Oliver went before the Tennessee Supreme Court three times. The government used the power of eminent domain to take land from people and companies who did not want to sell. Eminent domain is a right of the government under the Constitution. The government has the power to take a person's property away. However, there must be a good reason to do so. It must be for the good of the public. The government must pay the person a fair price.

CIVILIAN CONSERVATION CORPS (CCC)

By 1934, the government had enough land in the region to form the park. Congress passed an act to make it so. Great Smoky Mountains National Park became a reality. But the park was not ready to open. Much work had to be done first.

The park would need new roads, trails, and visitor centers. Buildings where people lived needed to be taken down. Crews of young men came to the park to do the work. They were part of the Civilian Conservation Corps, or CCC. The CCC was a government work program. It was part of President Franklin D. Roosevelt's New Deal.

The New Deal was a plan to help America's finances recover. The nation was struggling through the Great Depression, a period that lasted through the 1930s. During the Depression, money was very scarce, and there were few jobs to be had. The jobs in the Smokies came at a time when people desperately needed work. The crews worked under the supervision of the U.S. Army.

After several years of work in the region, the park was ready. On September 2, 1940, President Franklin D. Roosevelt stood at Newfound Gap. He looked out over the misty mountains and gave a short speech. Thanks to the hard work of many people, the Great Smoky Mountains was now a national park. People of the future would get to see this land in a natural state, much as the first settlers had.

⊘ OVERVIEW OF THE NATIONAL PARK

Today, Great Smoky Mountains National Park covers 521,086 acres. Look at it on a map and you'll see a green oasis free of towns. The park is sixty-five miles wide (from east to west) and twenty-five miles long (from north to south). It is one of the largest tracts of wilderness in the eastern United States. The Park Service does not maintain many roads. As a result, much of the park is free from cars. Instead, people can explore the park on foot. There are more than eight hundred miles of hiking trails.

Newfound Gap Road is the one major road in the park. It runs from Tennessee south into North Carolina. There is a visitor center as you enter the park from either direction. Sugarlands Visitor Center is two miles from Gatlinburg, while the Oconaluftee Visitor Center is just outside Cherokee, North Carolina. The visitor centers have lots of helpful information, and rangers are on hand to answer questions. Bookstores sell maps and guidebooks.

→ OCONALUFTEE MOUNTAIN FARM MUSEUM

Right next door to the Oconaluftee Visitor Center is the Mountain Farm Museum. In the 1950s, the National Park Service moved log buildings from around the park to this site. A farmhouse with a barn stands in a grassy clearing. In the spring, bright yellow forsythia flowers bloom near a weathered picket fence. There is the corncrib where settlers stored corn for the winter, and the smokehouse where pieces of meat dried slowly over a smoky fire.

A blacksmith would have heated iron in the fire to make it soften. Then he would have pounded it into shape, making nails and shoes for the horses. At the museum, rangers lead tours of buildings such as the blacksmith's shop. Some even dress in costume as settlers from a hundred years ago.

Each fall, they put on the Mountain Life Festival and demonstrate how settlers once lived. A

Great Smoky Mountains National Park - Mountain Farm Museum and Mingus Mill (U.S. National Park - Microsoft ...

File   Edit   View   Favorites   Tools   Help

Address   http://www.nps.gov/grsm/planyourvisit/mfm.htm   Go   Links

nps.gov
(home)

National Park Service
U.S. Department of the Interior

Great Smoky Mountains

National Park

search   go

◉ Search this park
○ Search nps.gov

view map   text size: A A A   printer friendly

PARK HOME
PLAN YOUR VISIT
  Directions
  Operating Hours & Seasons
  Fees & Reservations
  Things To Do
  Places To Go
    Visitor Centers
    Cades Cove
    Cataloochee
    Deep Creek
    Clingmans Dome
    Fontana Dam

Mountain Farm Museum and Mingus Mill

Read about the history of **Great Smoky Mountains National Park,** including the story of the Cherokee Indians and early settlers who lived there. This National Park Service site also points out places to visit in the park, such as the Mountain Farm Museum and Mingus Mill.

EDITOR'S CHOICE

huge pot bubbles away over an outdoor fire. People gather around to boil the juice of the sorghum cane into sweet, sticky molasses. Indoors, women cook in a kettle over a hearth fire. Life was full of hard work, but it had its charms. Sitting on the front porch, the settlers could soak up some truly breathtaking scenery.

➡ GRISTMILLS: GRINDING GRAIN FOR BREAD

Not far up the road from the museum is Mingus Mill. Mingus Mill is a gristmill that was built in the late 1800s and is still in operation today. Gristmills use big, heavy stone wheels to grind grains, like wheat and rye, into flour for bread. Settlers did not have access to stores where they could buy flour.

It takes a great deal of energy to make the millstones turn. Settlers wisely built mills near the fast-flowing creeks. In most mills, water flowed over a wooden waterwheel. As the wheel turned, a shaft turned the millstones. In this way, the settlers were able to use water to power their mills.

The Mingus Mill, however, used a more efficient steel turbine that was driven by waterpower. Corn was the settlers most important crop—it was an everyday food staple. The settlers ate cornmeal mush for breakfast and corn bread for dinner.[2] Mingus Mill is one of four gristmills in the park.

⊖ FONTANA DAM

Fontana Lake lies in the southwest of the park. It is a beautiful spot, and a great place to fish and boat. Yet one hundred years ago, it did not exist. The Tennessee Valley Authority (TVA) made this 11,700-acre lake.

A view of the aqueduct by Mingus Mill.

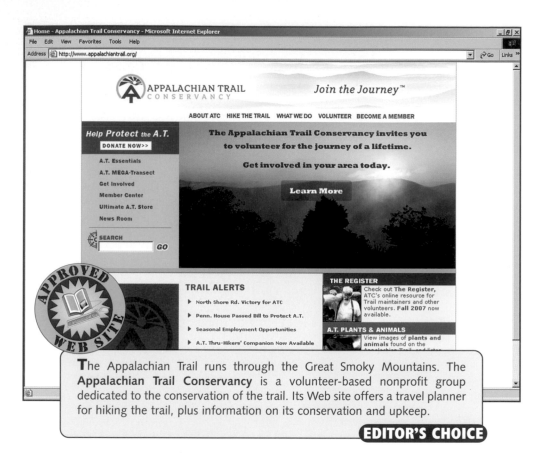

APPALACHIAN TRAIL
CONSERVANCY

Join the Journey™

ABOUT ATC   HIKE THE TRAIL   WHAT WE DO   VOLUNTEER   BECOME A MEMBER

Help **Protect** the A.T.

DONATE NOW>>

A.T. Essentials
A.T. MEGA-Transect
Get Involved
Member Center
Ultimate A.T. Store
News Room

SEARCH

GO

The Appalachian Trail Conservancy invites you
to volunteer for the journey of a lifetime.

Get involved in your area today.

Learn More

TRAIL ALERTS

▶ North Shore Rd. Victory for ATC

▶ Penn. House Passed Bill to Protect A.T.

▶ Seasonal Employment Opportunities

▶ A.T. Thru-Hikers' Companion Now Available

THE REGISTER

Check out The Register, ATC's online resource for Trail maintainers and other volunteers. **Fall 2007** now available.

A.T. PLANTS & ANIMALS

View images of **plants and animals** found on the Appalachian Trail and listed

The Appalachian Trail runs through the Great Smoky Mountains. The **Appalachian Trail Conservancy** is a volunteer-based nonprofit group dedicated to the conservation of the trail. Its Web site offers a travel planner for hiking the trail, plus information on its conservation and upkeep.

EDITOR'S CHOICE

APPROVED WEB SITE

In the 1940s, the TVA built a dam on the Little Tennessee River. The dam is 480 feet tall—the size of a city skyscraper! It is the tallest concrete dam east of the Rockies. The dam holds back the river's water. The water flooded the land and formed Fontana Lake. Water rushing through the dam drives giant turbines that generate electric power.

Today, there is a visitor center at the dam where you can learn the story of how the dam was built. This is where hikers on the Appalachian Trail—a hiking trail that runs from Georgia to Maine— enter Great Smoky Mountains National Park. They follow the trail as it goes right along the top of the mammoth dam.

PEAKS, BALDS, AND RIDGES

The Smokies are best known for black bears, waterfalls, and log cabins. Yet it is the mountains that the park is named for, and there is a good reason for that. The park features more than thirty miles of mountain ridgeline higher than five thousand feet (1,524 meters). The tallest peak, Clingmans Dome, is the third-highest mountain in the eastern United States.

What makes the Smokies so fascinating is the range of elevation. Even the valleys, the lowest areas, are eight hundred feet (243.8 meters) above sea level. The nearby mountain peaks are more than six thousand feet (1,828.8 meters) above sea level. Climbing one of these mountains takes you through many different climate zones. The only other way you could encounter so many different climates would be to hike the entire Appalachian Trail.

Dozens of mountains in the park are balds. Trees could grow at this elevation, but they do not. Some balds look like mountain meadows. It may be that settlers, who herded their animals here in the summer to graze on the oat grass, cleared them. With the animals gone, there is

A grassy bald, or mountaintop meadow, near the Appalachian Trail.

nothing to keep the fields mowed. On some balds, trees are beginning to take hold again.

Heath balds are nearly impossible to cross, unless someone has cut a trail. The shrubs grow so thick that no tree has a chance to grow. The heath balds are a beautiful sight in June, when the shrubs flower. The flame azaleas burst into orange and pink blooms. They smell as sweet as a bakeshop to a hungry hiker. The buds of the Catawba rhododendron unfurl into large, showy pink and purple flowers. The mountain laurel has clusters of smaller, pink and white cup-shaped flowers.

Cades Cove is a broad green valley, once home to about seven hundred settlers.

The nonprofit National Park Foundation helps to maintain and promote America's national parks. On its Web site you can plan a vacation, learn about the Junior Ranger program, and read and submit "inside information" based on park visits.

Access this Web site from http://www.myreportlinks.com

⊜ CADES COVE

Cades Cove is the most popular part of the park. It is a broad green valley surrounded by mountains. There was once a settlement here of seven hundred people. The park bought their land, and the people moved out. Some of the buildings still stand. Today an eleven-mile road runs through the cove. There are restored log houses, barns, churches, and the Cable Mill gristmill. Two mornings a week, the road is closed for car traffic. Only walkers and bicyclists are allowed, and the park runs horse-drawn hayride tours.

Chapter 4

A white-tailed buck (male deer) browses for food in a meadow of the park.

Plants and Animals of the Smokies

There are more than one hundred and thirty different species of trees that grow in the Smokies.[1] It is very rare for that many different kinds of trees to live in one area outside of the tropics. What makes the Smoky Mountains such a great place for trees? The answer, in part, is elevation. There is such a range of elevation, from the low valleys to the mountain peaks.

Some trees prefer to grow up high on the mountaintops. They do not mind the wind and the winter snow. Others prefer sun and warmth. They grow down in the valleys, where the weather is more stable. Some shade-loving trees grow on dark mountain slopes, while others need lots of water to thrive. They live along the banks of the creeks.

➔ A COVE FOREST

The Smoky Mountains are full of coves. A cove is a bowl-shaped valley.[2] The nearby mountain ridges protect the coves from harsh weather. The coves have deep soil, rich with nutrients. Mountain creeks feed the coves with a constant source of water.

As a result, lush forests with many different species grow in coves.

So many different kinds of trees and shrubs grow in this kind of forest that it is difficult to pick just a few to highlight. The most common large tree is the yellow buckeye, one of the first trees to leaf out each spring. It can grow up to ninety feet tall. Its branches spread wide.

The yellow poplar tree is one of the most common trees found in the park. It grows very quickly until it reaches the forest canopy. The canopy is the "roof" of the forest, formed by the branches of the tallest trees. With its leaves in the sun and its roots in the shade, this straight tall tree lives a long time. It can grow up to two hundred feet tall!

Temperate Rain Forest

The habitat found in the Great Smoky Mountains is a temperate rain forest. This Web site explains the ecology and natural resource management concerns related to the temperate rain forest environment.

Access this Web site from http://www.myreportlinks.com

Each year in the month of May, the tree awakes from its winter slumber and bursts into bloom. Its large flowers are greenish yellow and shaped like tulips. That is why many people call the yellow poplar by the name "tulip tree."

There is something magical about a shady grove of hemlock trees. The eastern hemlock is a tall evergreen with small flat needles. These majestic trees grow on dark, shaded slopes near streams. The air here is cool and damp.

→ AT HOME IN THE HEMLOCKS

Look carefully on the shady forest floor and you may spot an owl pellet. It does not look like much, just a grayish clump. Upon closer inspection, one can see the clump is made of hair and bones. The owl spits out the part of its diet that it cannot digest. Up in the hemlock branches overhead, the owl rests. When dusk falls, it will hunt for mice again.

A flowering shrub, the rosebay rhododendron, loves the shelter of the hemlocks. Rhododendrons crowd along the banks of the streams. Their showy white flowers are on display in June.

The largest hemlock in the United States grows in Great Smoky Mountain National Park. It stands at 165 feet tall. It measures sixteen feet around its trunk! A tree this size is extremely rare in the eastern United States today. Unfortunately a tiny insect, the hemlock woolly adelgid, is threatening

Eastern redbud trees show off their colorful pink spring blooms.

the hemlocks. More information may be found about the threat posed by this invasive exotic species in chapter 5.

⊜ SMALLER TREES OF THE UNDERSTORY

Some trees, like the flowering dogwood, never grow as high as the canopy. They live in the shade of the larger trees. These smaller trees form the forest understory, or the layer of trees between the canopy and the forest floor. The dogwood's flowers are tiny and yellow, surrounded by four large white leaves called bracts. A bract is a kind of leaf that looks more like a petal than a true leaf. In the fall, the dogwood's leaves turn bright orange. Birds like to eat its clusters of red berries.

The eastern redbud tree is the belle of the forest. In spring, its tiny pink flowers burst into bloom. The umbrella magnolia tree is pretty. Its white blossoms are bigger than your hand. But hold your nose—its flowers stink!

The Carolina silverbell is another spring beauty. Before the trees unfurl their leaves, the woods are gray and bare. The silverbell stands out, with its branches covered in tiny white flowers. Usually silverbell trees stay in the understory. They only grow to a height of thirty feet. Yet, under the right conditions, they can grow up into the canopy. The tallest silverbell in existence today is more than one hundred feet. Can you guess where it is? That's right—here in Great Smoky Mountains National Park.

→ ISLANDS OF NORTHERN BOREAL FORESTS

During the last ice age some ten thousand years ago, large masses of ice covered part of North America. As mentioned in chapter 2, these ice sheets, or glaciers, did not reach as far south as the Smoky Mountains. That is why the Smokies are much taller than the mountains in the North-east; they were never worn down by ice. But even though the glaciers did not come this far south, the climate was still much cooler than it is today.

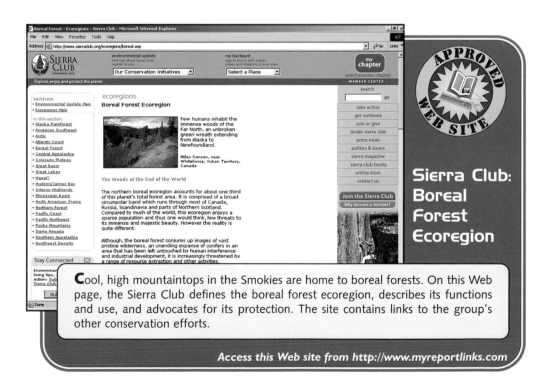

Cool, high mountaintops in the Smokies are home to boreal forests. On this Web page, the Sierra Club defines the boreal forest ecoregion, describes its functions and use, and advocates for its protection. The site contains links to the group's other conservation efforts.

Access this Web site from http://www.myreportlinks.com

It was cool enough that a boreal forest grew here. The word *boreal* means "from the north." Today boreal forests cover much of Canada and the far northern United States. Evergreens, like spruce and fir, are the trees that live in a boreal forest. As the climate warmed, spruce and fir trees could no longer live in the southern United States. The boreal forests died off in the South. They remain only on the highest mountaintops of the Smokies, where the climate is cooler. In these islands of boreal forest, red spruce and Fraser fir trees still dominate.

→ A HIDDEN VARIETY OF MAMMALS

While there are more than fifty kinds of mammals in the park, most of them stay hidden from sight. Visitors are most likely to see small mammals like squirrels and chipmunks. They scamper through the woods, scolding at hikers, as they collect nuts and seeds.

As the sun sets in the summer sky, herds of white-tailed deer come out of the woods. They browse on grass in meadows. Ever alert, they watch carefully for danger. If they sense a reason for alarm, they bound away, waving their white tails in the air. The males grow antlers each year, which they use to spar with one another. Females give birth to one or two spotted fawns in the spring. A fawn's spots help it blend in with the forest floor, keeping it safe from predators.

The shaggy black bear lumbers through the park in search of food. An adult male bear weighs two hundred pounds. Female bears weigh about one hundred and thirty pounds in the summer. By nature, a bear is shy and usually hides from people. Most park bears make dens in hollowed-out logs, and there they hibernate for the winter. Some den under tree root balls, in caves, or under dense undergrowth.

▲ *An adult male black bear may weigh about two hundred pounds. Most are shy and hide from visitors to the park.*

On warm winter days, a bear may wake up and come out of its den to forage for food. It is an omnivore, which means it will eat just about anything it can get its paws on. It mostly eats berries, acorns, roots, and leaves. It will also hunt for meat, especially in the spring when it is starving after its long sleep. Bear hunting and trapping is common in the South. The park, where hunting is illegal, is a refuge for the black bear.

A doglike animal crosses a field at a quick trot. Its pointy ears face forward, alert. It could be one of three different mammals. The beautiful red fox has a bright orange coat with a fluffy white-tipped tail. It eats bird eggs, mice, and voles. The fur of

North American Mammals: American Black Bear

The Smokies are home to about fifteen hundred black bears. This Web page from the Smithsonian National Museum of Natural History describes the species, its classification, and activities. It includes photographs, illustrations, and an audio clip of the black bear.

Access this Web site from http://www.myreportlinks.com

the gray fox is gray tinged with red. It can climb and hunt in trees. The larger coyote lives in packs. Coyotes are new to the Smoky Mountains. The first coyote in the park was identified in 1982.[3]

In the past, red wolves also lived here, but they were killed off in the 1800s. Mountain lions were once present, but they, too, no longer live in the park. The bobcat is the only wildcat that lives in the Smokies today. The bobcat is light brown and covered in spots. Its pointy ears have tufts of fur, and its short tail has a black tip. An adult grows more than three feet long—much larger than a house cat!

When an opossum is scared, it plays dead. The opossum has a pointy snout and a long, hairless tail. It belongs to a family of animals called marsupials. The female has a pouch on her stomach. After her tiny babies are born, she carries them in her pouch. Many marsupials, like the kangaroo, live in Australia. The opossum is the only one to live in North America.

⇒A Joyful Chorus

Stand still for a few minutes as you hike through the woods and listen. Before long, you will hear birds calling. More than two hundred and thirty kinds of birds have been spotted in the park.[4] Even in the depths of winter there is the sweet whistle of the black-capped chickadee. Blue jays jeer, *thief, thief.* The little nuthatch cries *ank-ank* as it clambers down the trunk of a tree upside down. A pileated woodpecker, with a red crest of feathers, peers out from a hole in a tree. Birds are everywhere, even on the mountain peaks.

TURKEY VULTURES AND RAVENS OVERHEAD

Large birds catch the wind under their wings and float along on the mountain thermals. From a distance, a turkey vulture looks regal as it soars through the air. Its wings form a V-shape. Up close, this large bird is not so pretty. It squats on the ground on large orange talons. Its pink head is bare of feathers. It eats carrion, or dead animals. While it soars, it is sniffing for the stench of rotting meat. The common raven, a large blackbird, lives in the spruce and fir forests on the mountains. Its call is a throaty croak. You can hear its large wings flap as it flies overhead.

At lower elevations, the forests are busy with small warblers. They flit and flutter in the shrubs. In the springtime, the male birds show off the brilliant colors of their breeding plumage (or feathers). By fall, their colors fade to brown or olive. Although their name would lead one to believe their songs are musical, some warbler species actually have thin, scratchy-sounding songs.

The ruffed grouse is a chicken-like bird. It will stay very still as you approach, hoping to go unseen. If you venture too close, it bursts into a panicked flight. The sudden explosion of noise puts your heart into your throat.

In the meadows, wild turkeys strut proudly with their families. They congregate under old apple trees in the fall, eating the fallen fruit. Barn swallows, with their forked tails, flit here and there. They are catching insects out of the air. In the evening, the wood thrush sings its curious

The black-capped chickadee is one of the more than two hundred and thirty bird species found in the park.

melody. It sounds different than anything else you have ever heard—a two-toned, flutelike call.

The eastern phoebe likes to build nests in old buildings. It seems to say its name in a raspy voice: *phoebe, phoebe.* Campers are sometimes kept awake at night by the loud call of the whip-poor-will. It seems to say its name rapidly over and over until you wish you had set your tent up somewhere else. Then suddenly it is gone.

⊜SALAMANDER CAPITAL OF THE WORLD

A salamander is an amphibian. Most of them grow just a few inches long. Some live their lives in the water; others live in the forest. They all need water to live, and the high rainfall of the Smokies suits them well. Even so, a visitor to the park might never see one. That is only because these little creatures are good at hiding. In fact, there are at least thirty species of salamander here.

Believe it or not, the biomass of all of the sala-manders in the park "exceeds that of all [the park's] birds and mammals combined."[5] Walking along on a rainy day, a hiker may see a patch of bright red on the forest floor. Most salamanders hide so that birds and other animals will not eat them. The red spotted newt does not bother. With its bright red skin, it is easy to see. Predators know to leave this newt alone. Its body contains a toxic chemical that makes them feel sick if eaten.

In the early spring, a loud chorus of chirps rises up from every pond and pool. The noise comes from the aptly named spring peepers. These tiny brown frogs are a sure sign that spring has come.

⊜REPTILES OF THE PARK

Reptiles have scaly skin, and lay eggs with hard shells. They're cold-blooded, so they need the sun to warm them. Turtles, snakes, and lizards are all reptiles that live in the Great Smoky Mountains. Most of the park's turtles live in the water. The eastern box turtle does not. It lives on land, and hikers can

Salamanders of Tennessee - Microsoft Internet Explorer

File   Edit   View   Favorites   Tools   Help

Address   http://www.state.tn.us/twra/tamp/salamanders.htm

Photo ©David Withers, TDEC-DNH

GREEN SALAMANDER
Aneides aeneus

A beautiful, rarely seen salamander (8 – 14 cm), the green salamander spends much of its time on sandstone, or sometimes limestone, rock faces with many crevices, or more rarely in trees or under the loose bark of fallen timber. This salamander has a black base color with a yellowish-green, lichen-like pattern upon the back. It has a flattened body, long legs and square toe tips, all adaptations for living on cliffs. Females of this species deposit their eggs in moist crevices in the rock face and will actively protect their eggs from small predators and fungus. The range of this species is rather limited in Tennessee, being confined mainly to the Cumberland Mountain, Highland Rim and Cumberland Plateau physiographic provinces.

Photo ©Stephen G. Tilley

SEEPAGE SALAMANDER
Desmognathus aeneus

One of the two smallest salamanders in Tennessee (3.8 – 5.7 cm), the seepage salamander has a yellowish to reddish-brown wavy, or sometimes straight, stripe going down the back. They often have a dark "Y" behind the head and extending onto the midline of the back either in a line or series of dots; they may also have a light circular patch on the top of each thigh. Some individuals may bear a very faint herringbone pattern upon the back, similar to the pygmy salamander. These salamanders live in and around seepage areas and near streams in moist or wet leaf litter, under logs or other surface objects and in moss mats. They are found only in the southeastern corner of the state along the Ten... Carolina border. The seepage salamander is listed in Ten... Management."

APPROVED WEB SITE

Great Smoky Mountain National Park is known as the "Salamander Capital of the World." Learn all about the **Salamanders of Tennessee** on this Web page from the Tennessee Wildlife Resources Agency. Photographs and text about dozens of salamander species are provided here.

spot this little turtle as it marches slowly through the woods. It stops to warm itself in a patch of sunlight. Its shell is black or brown and covered in orange, yellow, or green marks. Even the box turtle's head and legs have a colorful design.

There are two venomous snakes in this area. The timber rattlesnake will shake the rattle on the end of its tail if it feels threatened. The smaller northern copperhead is harder to spot. It blends in with the dried leaves on the forest floor. Both of these snakes carry deadly venom in their fangs, so give them a wide berth!

A juvenile orange salamander clings to a tree.

The park is also home to many harmless snakes. One of the most common is the northern water snake. It swims in the water, where it catches fish and tadpoles to eat. A little garter snake may give you a start as it slithers by.

Lizards look a bit like big salamanders, but they have scales and claws. With their claws, they can move quite fast and even climb trees. In the Great Smoky Mountains, there are several kinds of small lizards. The northern fence lizards are just six inches long. Local people call them bluebellies because they have blue markings on their underside.

One of the largest lizards found in the park is the broadhead skink. The males can grow over a foot long, and have brown bodies and bright orange heads. The largest lizard found in the park is the Eastern slender glass lizard. This is a legless lizard that looks like a snake. They can be over forty inches in length! This type of lizard is very rare in the park, although one was found in Cades Cove.

Chapter

5

Part of the Great Smoky Mountains seen through a blue haze.

The Future of the Great Smoky Mountains

Even on a clear summer day, the Smoky Mountains are hazy. Some of the haze comes from water in the air. It covers the mountainsides with a thin cloud layer. All the water in the air can make it hard to see very far.

Some haze comes from trees during respiration—they emit volatile organic compounds (VOCs) that give off a blue haze. This gives the Blue Ridge Mountains their name. Most people do not mind the haze—it is part of the charm of the view. Yet the haze is rapidly growing worse, and that is a problem. The culprit is air pollution, or smog. Tiny particles hang in the air and block the scenery.

→ ARE THE SMOKIES TOO SMOKY?

No matter how hard the National Park

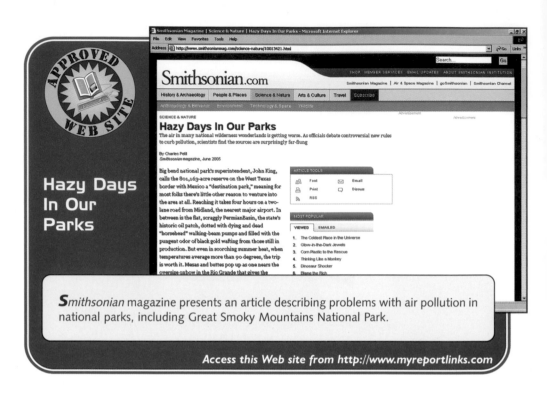

APPROVED WEB SITE

Hazy Days
In Our
Parks

Search...   Go

Smithsonian.com

SHOP   MEMBER SERVICES   EMAIL UPDATES   ABOUT SMITHSONIAN INSTITUTION

Smithsonian Magazine | Air & Space Magazine | goSmithsonian | Smithsonian Channel

History & Archaeology   People & Places   Science & Nature   Arts & Culture   Travel   Subscribe

Anthropology & Behavior   Environment   Technology & Space   Wildlife

SCIENCE & NATURE

Hazy Days In Our Parks

The air in many national wilderness wonderlands is getting worse. As officials debate controversial new rules to curb pollution, scientists find the sources are surprisingly far-flung

By Charles Pelt
Smithsonian magazine, June 2005

Big bend national park's superintendent, John King, calls the 801,163-acre reserve on the West Texas border with Mexico a "destination park," meaning for most folks there's little other reason to venture into the area at all. Reaching it takes four hours on a two-lane road from Midland, the nearest major airport. In between is the flat, scraggly PermianBasin, the state's historic oil patch, dotted with dying and dead "horsehead" walking-beam pumps and filled with the pungent odor of black gold wafting from those still in production. But even in scorching summer heat, when temperatures average more than 90 degrees, the trip is worth it. Mesas and buttes pop up as one nears the oversize oxbow in the Rio Grande that gives the

ARTICLE TOOLS

Font   Email
Print   Discuss
RSS

MOST POPULAR

VIEWED   EMAILED

1.   The Coldest Place in the Universe
2.   Glow-in-the-Dark Jewels
3.   Corn Plastic to the Rescue
4.   Thinking Like a Monkey
5.   Dinosaur Shocker
6.   Blame the Rich

Smithsonian magazine presents an article describing problems with air pollution in national parks, including Great Smoky Mountains National Park.

Access this Web site from http://www.myreportlinks.com

overhead; it is constantly moving. Most of the air pollution is not generated in the park, but comes from power plants.[1] The power plants burn coal for fuel. When the coal burns, it releases energy. The energy becomes the electricity we use every day. But the coal also releases smoke that includes sulfur and nitrogen compounds. The smoke rises up through tall smokestacks, where it becomes part of the air.

Winds carry the polluted air away. When the polluted winds hit the Smoky Mountains, the air cools down. Much of it falls to the ground as rain or snow. Or it forms a fog which settles over the trees. The polluted fog wears away at the trees' leaves and needles. People sometimes call polluted rain "acid rain." It is much more acidic than normal rain. Vinegar and lemon juice are familiar acids. If something is highly acidic, it can burn. Acid rain burns plants and trees.

When the acid rain enters the ground, it reacts with the metals in the soil. The metals leach out, or come loose from, the soil. Trees and plants then soak up the metals—especially aluminum—through their roots. These metals belong in the ground, not in the plants. They are toxic to the plants. The plants grow weak, and it is easier for diseases and fungi to infect them.[2]

Acid rain also changes the makeup of the rivers and groundwater. There is some good news in all

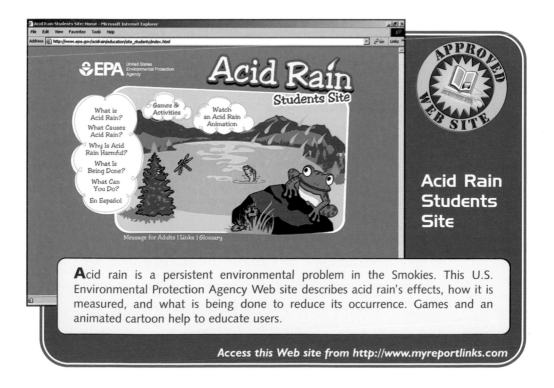

Acid Rain Students Site

Acid rain is a persistent environmental problem in the Smokies. This U.S. Environmental Protection Agency Web site describes acid rain's effects, how it is measured, and what is being done to reduce its occurrence. Games and an animated cartoon help to educate users.

Access this Web site from http://www.myreportlinks.com

this. People have the knowledge and technology to prevent air pollution and acid rain. Americans must urge our lawmakers to pass laws to curb acid rain. And practicing conservation—such as turning off lights that are not needed—can also help so that we don't need as much electricity.

⊖CAR EMISSIONS

Power plants are not the only cause of air pollution. Cars and trucks are another big contributor. They run on gasoline. Like coal, gasoline creates lots of energy when it is burned. It also creates the smelly exhaust that shoots out of a car's tailpipe. The exhaust becomes part of the air. On days when air pollution is high, it is difficult to breathe. It is not safe, especially for children, the elderly, and people with asthma.

Millions of cars drive through Great Smoky Mountains National Park each year. People drive up over Newfound Gap Road to see the views—it is one of the highlights of the park. But the views are not so wonderful these days. Those cars are part of the problem.

So far, the park service has not had the power to limit the number of cars in the park. However, it is moving forward with alternate plans, which include limiting cars for Cades Cove. Even if the park service decides to offer shuttles, though, that solution will not solve the larger problem. Air quality is a major issue that the entire nation needs to address soon.

⊜ BOARS ON THE LOOSE

Along stream banks in the Smokies, plants are uprooted. Large patches of soil in a meadow are torn up. It almost looks as if someone has come through with a plow.

The culprit is a wild hog, or boar. It looks like a pig with tusks. It is covered in bristly hair.

A wild hog can grow to weigh up to two hundred pounds. It grubs through the dirt with its

▽ *Wild boars, or hogs, are not native to the area of the park and run loose in it. They tear up the ground and create problems for native species by eating their food sources.*

snout in search of food. Wild hogs eat roots, insects, salamanders, snails, and bird eggs.[3] Although the hogs are wild, they are not native to the area. They come from Europe. Sport hunters brought the boars to America in 1912 to stock their game preserves.

The trouble began when the hogs escaped from a nearby game preserve in 1920. They settled in Great Smoky Mountains National Park. There are no natural predators that hunt wild hogs. People are not allowed to hunt in the park, and the number of hogs quickly multiplied.

It was not long before there were too many hogs in the park. One female can give birth to

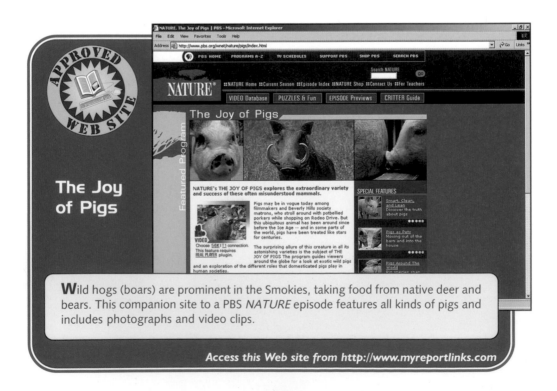

Wild hogs (boars) are prominent in the Smokies, taking food from native deer and bears. This companion site to a PBS *NATURE* episode features all kinds of pigs and includes photographs and video clips.

Access this Web site from http://www.myreportlinks.com

three to eight piglets as often as twice a year. Not only do the hogs tear up the ground, they also eat acorns and nuts—taking that food away from the native deer and bears. Park staff realized something would have to be done. After all, part of the park's mission is to protect native species. They wanted to rid the park of the hogs.

In the 1950s, the staff began to trap and shoot the hogs. Local hunters were upset. They did not want the boars killed. They wanted the park staff to trap the animals and release them outside the park.[4] Either way, getting rid of the hogs has proved difficult to do. Wild hogs are fast runners, and they are good at evading hunters. In 2003, the National Park Service estimated there are five to six hundred hogs living in Great Smoky Mountains National Park.[5]

Do Not Feed the Bears

There are approximately fifteen hundred black bears living in Great Smoky Mountain National Park. Black bears usually stay away from people, and people are wise to stay away from them, too. A black bear is very strong. It lumbers slowly through the woods. It pauses to eat some berries or to lift rotted logs to look for grubs. Do not let it fool you—a black bear can run quite quickly when it wants to. A mother bear can be especially irritable. She is anxious to protect her young. She is also hungry, as she must eat more food to make milk for her babies.

In the 1960s, a visitor to Great Smoky Mountain National Park would have seen bears approach people to beg for food. People gave bears handouts. They laughed as bears stole food from their picnic lunches. Tourists knew that they could get a good picture of a bear by luring it out in to the open with food.

FEEDING THE BEARS IS A CRIME

The bears were quick learners. They stopped foraging for food in the wild. Instead, they harassed people. They searched cars, backpacks, and campgrounds for food. The bears became a serious threat to people. Sadly, many had to be shot.

Today there are laws that prohibit feeding the bears. It is a crime subject to fines of up to five thousand dollars and jail times of up to six months. The Park Service does its part to teach campers about bears. At backcountry campsites (campsites that people reach by backpacking), there are cable and pulley systems that campers must use to raise up their bags of food at night. At frontcountry sites (where people camp beside their cars), campers are required to keep their food in a closed vehicle. Certain other campgrounds (such as Cades Cove and Balsam

Mountain) have food storage lockers for campers to share.

➡ A SECOND CHANCE FOR ELK AND OTTER

Centuries ago, bands of elk roamed through these mountains. Like deer, elk have hooves and antlers. But an elk is larger than a white-tailed deer. Its antlers are larger—nearly four feet across. It has tan fur, except around its neck and head where the fur is dark brown. An elk stands five feet tall at the shoulder.

By the late 1700s, the elk were gone. People had hunted all the native elk for meat. In 2001, the National Park Service tried to bring elk back to the park. Under the Endangered Species Act, the Park Service tries to help endangered animals, if people are the reason they are in danger. Each year, the park staff released some elk. The project seems to be working. Today, the herd is up to seventy animals. Several elk have successfully given birth to calves in the wild.

The river otter loves to play. This brown furry animal waddles on its short legs. It slides down the riverbank on its stomach. Plop! It swims through the water with skill. Its webbed feet make great paddles.

Like the elk, the otter is another native to the Smokies that was driven off by people. Hunters

Once native to the Smokies, the river otter was driven off by hunters and loggers. This threatened species was reintroduced to the park in the 1980s.

North American River Otter

Animal Fact Sheets - Microsoft Internet Explorer

File   Edit   View   Favorites   Tools   Help

Address http://www.zoo.org/factsheets/river_otter/riverOtter.html   Go   Links

North American River Otter
(*Lontra canadensis*)

threatened species

Classification and Range
Otters belong to the family Mustelidae, which also includes badgers, mink, martens, skunks, weasels and wolverines. Otters are classified under the subfamily Lutrinae, which has a total of 13 species in seven genera.*

North American river otters are found throughout Alaska, Canada and the contiguous United States.

North America

printable version   video clip   Adopt me!   more

Habitat	Length	Weight	Life Span	Diet
North American river otters live in a variety of habitats, but they spend most of their time in or near streams, rivers, lakes and marshes. They often build a den or a burrow in their home	Adult length, with tail: 2.5-5 feet (76-152 cm)	Adult weight: 10-30 pounds (4.5-13.6 kg)	Life span in the wild is 10 years; up to 18-20 years in zoos	**In the wild:** Birds, crabs, crayfish, fish, frogs, rodents, turtles, and aquatic invertebrates. Otters eat whatever is readily available and easiest to catch.

The Woodland Park Zoo presents extensive information on the North American river otter. Topics covered include its classification, habitat, life span, behavior, and more. Watch a video, and learn how you can help this threatened species.

Access this Web site from http://www.myreportlinks.com

prized it for its fur. Loggers used the streams to float logs to the mills. They disturbed much of the otter's habitat. In the 1980s, the river otter was reintroduced to the park. Today it can be found in most of the larger streams in the park.

➔ THREATS TO THE FOREST

The chestnut was once the king of the Appalachian forest. This magnificent tree grew to be one hundred feet tall, and its branches spread wide. In the spring, its white blossoms filled the tree like snow. In the autumn, the tree dropped thousands of chestnuts. It provided food for birds, deer, bear, and squirrels. Even people gathered the chestnuts to eat.

But in the 1920s, the chestnut trees began to die off. They were under attack by a chestnut blight fungus that spread rapidly. Within a few years, all the chestnuts were dead. Lumber companies cut as many as they could.

The fungus was so destructive because it was not native to America. The trees had no resistance to it. The fungus came from Asia on some nursery plants shipped to New York. Young chestnut trees still grow in the park today. They sprout up from the stumps of old chestnut trees. Unfortunately, the blight kills the young trees before they can make seeds.

⇒ A DESTRUCTIVE INSECT

To see the damage a tiny insect can do, follow the Appalachian Trail through the Smokies. As the trail approaches the peak of Clingmans Dome, it passes through a ghost forest. In the last century, there was a healthy fir forest here. Today, dead and dying fir trees creak in the wind. The balsam woolly adelgid caused this destruction. This tiny insect is not from this part of the world. It came to America from Europe one hundred years ago.[6]

The fir trees in North America were ill-prepared for the adelgid. The adelgid has killed off nearly all of the balsam and Fraser fir trees in the Smokies. It sucks the sap from a fir tree for food. As it eats, it

▲ Eastern hemlock trees show the results of infestation by the woolly adelgid. The insect sucks the sap from the tree's needles, which causes them to fall off. Without their needles, the trees die off.

releases a toxin into the tree. The toxin destroys the wood, and the tree dies. The adelgids eventually destroy their only source of food.

It is sad that yet another kind of adelgid has turned up in the Smokies. People first began spotting the hemlock woolly adelgid within the last ten years. The insect covers itself with a waxy white wool-like coating. Infested hemlock trees can be identified by tiny cotton-like balls at the base of their needles. The adelgid sucks the sap from the needles. This eventually causes the needles to drop off, and without needles the hemlock trees starve to death.

A National Park Service employee spraying Eastern hemlock trees in Cades Cove with oil designed to suffocate the woolly adelgid.

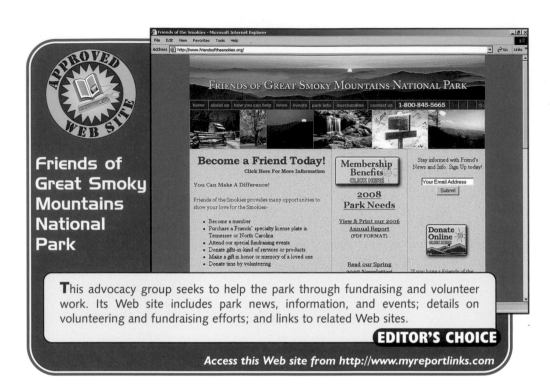

FRIENDS OF GREAT SMOKY MOUNTAINS NATIONAL PARK

home | about us | how you can help | news | events | park info | merchandise | contact us | 1-800-845-5665

Become a Friend Today!
Click Here For More Information

You Can Make A Difference!

Friends of the Smokies provides many opportunities to show your love for the Smokies-

• Become a member
• Purchase a Friends' specialty license plate in Tennessee or North Carolina
• Attend our special fundraising events
• Donate gifts-in-kind of services or products
• Make a gift in honor or memory of a loved one
• Donate time by volunteering

Membership Benefits
CLICK HERE

2008 Park Needs

View & Print our 2006 Annual Report (PDF FORMAT)

Read our Spring

Stay informed with Friend's News and Info. Sign Up today!

Your Email Address
Submit

Donate Online
CLICK HERE

Friends of Great Smoky Mountains National Park

This advocacy group seeks to help the park through fundraising and volunteer work. Its Web site includes park news, information, and events; details on volunteering and fundraising efforts; and links to related Web sites.

EDITOR'S CHOICE

Access this Web site from http://www.myreportlinks.com

Scientists are searching for ways to save the hemlock trees. They fear that the hemlocks may die off in large numbers.[7] No one understands what impact this might have on the park since there are more than ninety thousand acres of hemlock there. The park is using three different treatments to kill the adelgids, including spraying and releasing predator beetles (which prey on the adelgids).[8]

Hemlock groves are shady and cool. Many animals make their homes there. Hemlocks also protect streams, keeping them cool for the fish that swim there. People can help in the effort by making donations and buying T-shirts that say "Save the Hemlocks."

→LEAVE NO TRACE

The national parks have a rule: Leave No Trace. Rangers teach people to take only photographs and leave only footprints. Imagine if every visitor to the park dug up a plant and took it home. More than 9 million plants would leave the park—each year! That is why it is against the law to take things from the park.

Poachers are people who hunt animals, catch fish, or harvest plants when it is against the law to do so. In the Smokies, one thing people poach is wild ginseng. Ginseng is a plant that grows on the shady forest floor. It is the Cherokee tradition to use ginseng as medicine.[9] Its root is worth up to

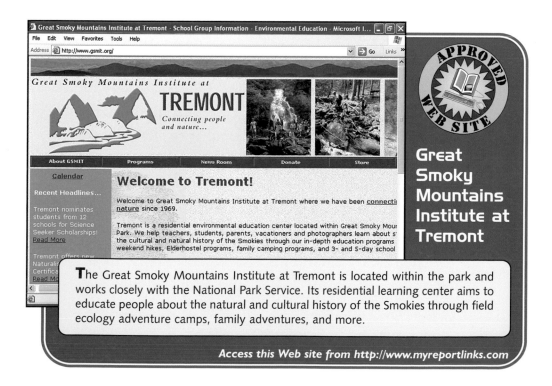

The Great Smoky Mountains Institute at Tremont is located within the park and works closely with the National Park Service. Its residential learning center aims to educate people about the natural and cultural history of the Smokies through field ecology adventure camps, family adventures, and more.

Access this Web site from http://www.myreportlinks.com

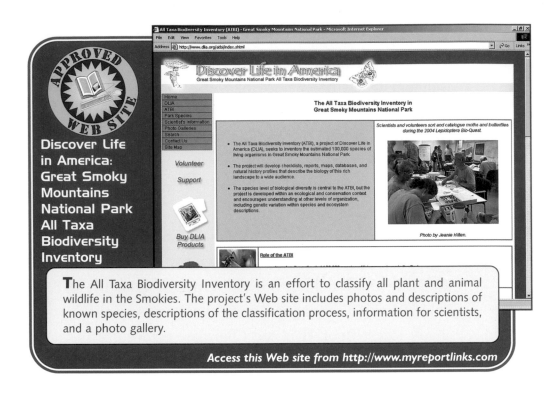

Discover Life in America: Great Smoky Mountains National Park All Taxa Biodiversity Inventory

The All Taxa Biodiversity Inventory is an effort to classify all plant and animal wildlife in the Smokies. The project's Web site includes photos and descriptions of known species, descriptions of the classification process, information for scientists, and a photo gallery.

Access this Web site from http://www.myreportlinks.com

$375 per pound.[10] By digging up the root, poachers destroy the plant.

The people of the United States essentially own Great Smoky Mountains National Park. By paying taxes, they are contributing to the costs of taking care of the park. It is the job of the U.S. Congress to decide how much money to give the national parks. It is not always enough. That is where the Great Smoky Mountains Association steps in. It publishes and sells books and maps about the Smokies. The proceeds, as well as the group's donations and volunteer efforts, help to fund education and wildlife management in the park.

Friends of the Great Smoky Mountains National Park is another group that helps the park. It works with the park to raise extra funds and public awareness. For example, the group worked with the states of Tennessee and North Carolina. Now people in those two states can pay a little extra for a special license plate. Then each state gives part of the fee to benefit the park.

Great Smoky Mountains Institute at Tremont is a nonprofit organization that serves more than four thousand schoolchildren each year, and annually provides more than $1 million in environmental educational services. Its residential learning center is located within the park.

ATBI: All Taxa Biodiversity Inventory

Groups of scientists trek through the forest, clipboards in hand. Their goal is to catalog every single plant and animal in the park. They want to understand life in the Smokies, and how it is changing. Hundreds of scientists are working together on the All Taxa Biodiversity Inventory (ATBI). Volunteers are helping, too. They believe it will take fifteen years or more to complete. Already the project has found hundreds of new species of life. The results will help the park service as it strives to protect the park for the future.

Chapter

6

Blossoming pear trees line a road leading to the Smokies.

Things to Do and See in the Smokies

The best way to see the sights of Great Smoky Mountains National Park is to take a walk. There are hundreds of miles of trails to choose from, and they explore all types of terrain. There are flat, meandering paths, while paved walkways lead to waterfalls. Trails with steep switchbacks zigzag up steep mountainsides.

No matter what your skill level, there is a hike for you to enjoy. If you walk quietly and keep alert, you will see some wildlife. Even though there are hundreds of thousands of people in the park, most of them never venture farther than a hundred yards from their car. Even so, you probably will not be alone on the trail. Chances are you'll meet plenty of folks, from all over the country and

Clouds mix with mountaintops in this autumn view of the Smokies.

Hikers often stop to chat as they pass one another. They tell each other how much farther it is to the peak or that the scenic view is worth the side trip. Fellow hikers are a great source of information. If you persevere and push yourself to climb to the mountaintop, you will be rewarded. The views are out of this world. Rugged peaks stretch ahead for miles and miles.

⇒ BIKE, SNOWSHOE OR SKI

A long, leisurely bicycle ride may be more your style. There are bikes for rent at Cades Cove. A bike is a great way to get exercise and explore at the same time. To protect the plants, stay on the trail. The Parson Branch Road, near the Cades Cove Visitor Center, goes through tunnels of rosebay rhododendrons. In mid-June they are in bloom with white flowers.

During the winter, it rarely snows down in the valleys. If it does, it soon melts away. The mountains, on the other hand, get several feet of snow. The mountain roads are closed down for the winter season. It is too bad for people in cars, but great if you like snow sports. Dress in warm layers, pack a thermos of hot cocoa, and strap on the snowshoes or cross-country skis.

Winter is a good time to view wildlife. The trees are bare of leaves and you can see far through the woods. Everything is hushed under the blanket of snow. It is easy to hear birds calling. Animal tracks show up clearly in the snow, too.

Horseback riding is a popular sport in the Smokies. More than five hundred miles of trails are open to horseback riders. People can rent a mount at one of three sites in the park. Guides will lead you on a trek through the woods to view a rushing waterfall. Or bring your own horse on a camping trip. The park has campsites designated for people with horses. There is no grazing allowed, so plan to bring food for your horse. If you are not a rider but still like horses, try a carriage ride around Cades Cove.

There is no hunting allowed in the park. You can catch fish—and with more than seventy different kinds of fish living in the park's streams, it is a popular activity. But there are a few rules that must be followed. First, you must apply for a fishing permit from a nearby town. You cannot use live bait. And make sure you know what brook trout look like. You are allowed to catch and keep brook trout from most streams in the park if they measure more than seven inches in length. But if they're smaller than that, you must let the fish go unharmed.

WHITEWATER RAFTING OUTSIDE THE PARK

The National Park Service does not recommend swimming or tubing in the park. Every year there

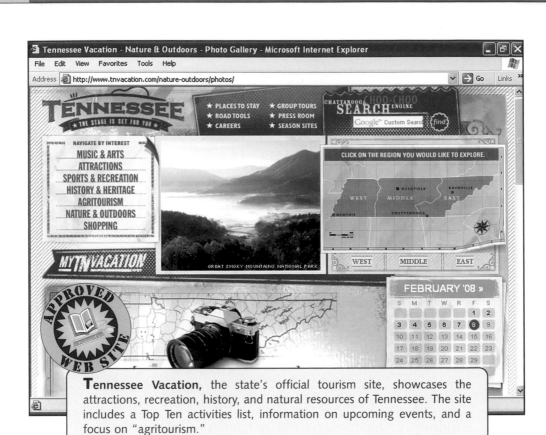

Tennessee Vacation - Nature & Outdoors - Photo Gallery - Microsoft Internet Explorer

File   Edit   View   Favorites   Tools   Help

Address   http://www.tnvacation.com/nature-outdoors/photos/   Go   Links

TENNESSEE
★ THE STAGE IS SET FOR YOU ★

★ PLACES TO STAY   ★ GROUP TOURS
★ ROAD TOOLS   ★ PRESS ROOM
★ CAREERS   ★ SEASON SITES

CHATTANOOGA CHOO-CHOO
SEARCH ENGINE
Google™ Custom Search   find

NAVIGATE BY INTEREST
MUSIC & ARTS
ATTRACTIONS
SPORTS & RECREATION
HISTORY & HERITAGE
AGRITOURISM
NATURE & OUTDOORS
SHOPPING

CLICK ON THE REGION YOU WOULD LIKE TO EXPLORE.

NASHVILLE   KNOXVILLE
WEST   MIDDLE   EAST
MEMPHIS   CHATTANOOGA

MY TN VACATION

GREAT SMOKY MOUNTAINS NATIONAL PARK

WEST   MIDDLE   EAST

APPROVED WEB SITE

FEBRUARY '08 »

S	M	T	W	R	F	S
					1	2
3	4	5	6	7	8	9
10	11	12	13	14	15	16
17	18	19	20	21	22	23
24	25	26	27	28	29	

Tennessee Vacation, the state's official tourism site, showcases the attractions, recreation, history, and natural resources of Tennessee. The site includes a Top Ten activities list, information on upcoming events, and a focus on "agritourism."

are visitors with water-related injuries. A much safer thrill is to try whitewater rafting at a nearby facility. A professional guide will steer as you help paddle. Getting splashed as your raft rides the waves is all part of the fun. The Nantahala River is just south of the park. Its rushing waters squeeze through a small gorge. The hills rise steeply on either side. It is also a nice place for a picnic while you watch others tackle the river. At any given time, a helmeted kayaker tries to get up the nerve to take on the foaming white water.

⇢SLEEPING UNDER THE STARS

There are many hotels, motels, and inns to stay in nearby the park. If you want to truly experience the wilderness, sleep in a tent out under the stars. There are ten campgrounds in the park. Campsites cost only a small fee. Each one has a picnic table and a fire pit. Bring your own sleeping bag, tent, and graham crackers for making s'mores.

At the large campgrounds, like Elkmont, Cades Cove, and Cosby, there are lots of campers and plenty to do. You can hear a ranger tell ghost stories around the campfire or go on a wildflower walk. Park rangers also give talks about wildlife and the history of the park.

If you came to the park to escape the crowds, try a smaller campground. At Big Creek, there are only twelve tent sites. Cataloochee Campground is also small and quite remote. There you can pitch your tent under the shade of the hemlock trees. Lying in your sleeping bag, you will fall asleep to the sound of the nearby creek babbling as it flows over the rocks.

Or you can really avoid the crowds and hike to a backcountry campsite. Although they are free, you will need to get a permit to stay at a backcountry site. Most sites are rustic, and you pitch your tent on the ground. There are shelters at some backcountry sites located along the Appalachian Trail, as well as a few others such as

Laurel Gap. All sites are located near a water source, be it a bubbling mountain spring or a fast-running stream.

⊜ LeConte Lodge

There is only one place where the public can sleep in a bed in the park: LeConte Lodge. Built in 1924, it

A view of Mount LeConte, the third-highest peak in the Smokies.

is perched like an eagle's nest high on the top of Mount LeConte. A private concession runs the lodge. At 6,593 feet (2,009.5 meters), Mount LeConte is the third-highest peak in the Smokies. Guests need reservations and must hike one of six trails up the mountain to reach the lodge.

LeConte Lodge is no luxury inn, but a rustic retreat. There are old-fashioned washbasins rather than showers. At night, kerosene lanterns glow with a soft yellow light. There is no electricity. When the sun goes down and the wind picks up, guests gather to warm themselves by the woodstove. The sleeping cabins have bunk beds. The kitchen staff cooks meals, and everyone eats together around the table.

Llamas carry up supplies several times a week. That's right; there are llamas in the Smokies! Llamas are

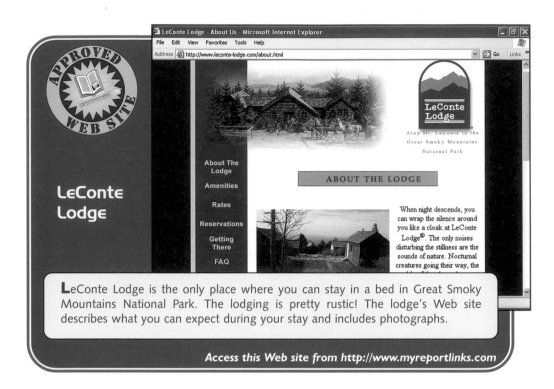

LeConte Lodge is the only place where you can stay in a bed in Great Smoky Mountains National Park. The lodging is pretty rustic! The lodge's Web site describes what you can expect during your stay and includes photographs.

Access this Web site from http://www.myreportlinks.com

pack animals that are adept at climbing mountains. They are native to the rocky Andes mountains of South America.

→ DISCOVERING BYGONE DAYS

Once, thousands of people lived in small farming villages in the Smokies. The government bought them out when the park was created. They took most of the buildings down to return the land to its natural state. Still, there are signs of the park's past. A white clapboard church stands on a hill, guarding a simple graveyard. A gristmill with a waterwheel grinds corn into cornmeal. A settler's log cabin sits in a clearing. It is surrounded by a gray weathered fence.

All in all, there are seventy-eight buildings still standing from days gone by. Many of them are at Cades Cove. Old Timer's Day is held there each spring in May. People who remember living in the park come back to reminisce. They bring their children and their grandchildren. Others come to enjoy the fun and hear about life in the old days. The festival begins with a church sermon, followed by music, feasting, and dancing.

Cataloochee holds its Homecoming Day in the autumn, as the trees begin to turn color. Cataloochee

Gatlinburg, Tennessee: Gateway to the Smokies

Gatlinburg, Tennessee, is located near the Sugarlands Visitor Center of the Great Smoky Mountains National Park. The official tourism site spotlights its attractions and available outdoor activities. It also includes a section on history and heritage.

Access this Web site from http://www.myreportlinks.com

was the largest settlement before the park was founded, with more than twelve hundred residents. Now Cataloochee is remote and difficult to get to. It gets far fewer visitors than Cades Cove. Old-timers and their families come to visit the land that was once their home. They decorate the graves in the cemeteries and remember the past. The church bell at Palmer Chapel tolls for any old-timers who have died in the past year.[1]

➡ BRIGHT LIGHTS OF GATLINBURG

The bright lights of Gatlinburg are sure to dazzle your eyes if you have been camping for a few days. The city is packed with tourists headed for a game of mini-golf or a ride on a waterslide or roller coaster. That is not all there is to the town. It is famous for keeping alive the old-time mountain crafts.

At the Arrowmont School of Arts and Crafts, you can learn about quilting, basketry, or furniture making. The school offers workshops where you can learn to make an old-fashioned twig broom or a clay pot.

The Roaring Fork Motor Nature Trail leads from town back into the park. It is a six-mile loop with lots of places to stop and explore. Roam through a grove of huge hemlock trees. Listen to the sound of the splashing water as it cascades over the rocks.

During the winter, tourists can take advantage of Ober Gatlinburg, Tennessee's only ski resort. It offers eight slopes for skiing and snowboarding. There is also an indoor ice skating rink.

⊘ EXPLORE CHEROKEE HISTORY AND CULTURE

From Gatlinburg, Newfound Gap Road climbs east up through the mountains. It leads to the town of Cherokee, on the North Carolina side. Cherokee is part of the Qualla Boundary Lands. It is the home of the Eastern Band of the Cherokee Indians.

The Museum of the Cherokee Indian is here. Its new, 3-million-dollar exhibits are state of the art. They tell the story of how the Paleo-Indians hunted mastodons with spears. The exhibits show American-Indians of the Woodland era as they begin to grow crops. Holograms bring a shaman to life. He tells about the life of the early Cherokee.

At the Oconaluftee Indian Village, people can walk around a replica of an eighteenth-century Cherokee village. Rough cabins and a council house stand in a forest clearing. Modern-day Cherokee guides show visitors around and demonstrate the ways of the past. They make dugout canoes, carve blowguns, and weave baskets. In the summer months, actors perform an outdoor play, *Unto These Hills.* It tells the story of the Cherokee and the forced march on the Trail of Tears.

Discover
Bluegrass

Bluegrass evolved from "mountain music," which was native to the area around the Smokies. This Web site defines the style and provides its history. It also features top performers and a band directory.

Access this Web site from http://www.myreportlinks.com

⇒ BLUEGRASS, CLOGGING, AND WILD ONIONS

The early pioneers had to entertain themselves. Many who settled in the coves were of Scotch-Irish stock. They sang the songs of their homeland, the British Isles. Some families were lucky enough to have a fiddle and someone who could play along. Over the years, mountain music evolved into bluegrass music.

Bluegrass has a sound all its own. The singers have high, lonesome-sounding voices. The harmonies are complicated. The music tends to be fast. Fingers fly as musicians pluck at the strings. The fiddle is still at the heart of the music, but many other instruments have joined the band. Bluegrass musicians strum banjos and guitars. They play dulcimers, mandolins, and Dobros.

How do you dance along to bluegrass? Why, you clog, of course! As in Irish dancing, the upper body stays mostly still. The focus is on the legs and feet of the dancer. Like the music, the steps are fast and complicated. Clogging is so popular that most schools here have competitive clogging teams. The cloggers take the stage as a group. Their shoes tap out a rhythm as they hit the floor. They often wear traditional dress. Mountain music and dance is everywhere in the Smokies.

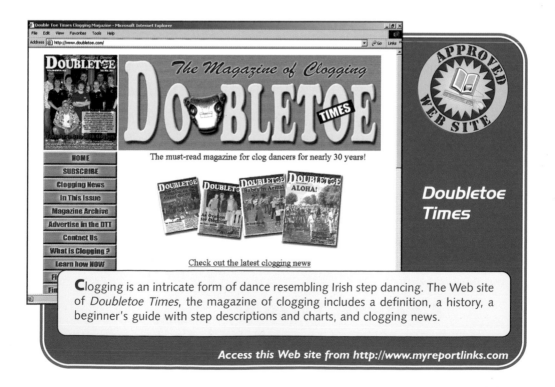

Clogging is an intricate form of dance resembling Irish step dancing. The Web site of *Doubletoe Times*, the magazine of clogging includes a definition, a history, a beginner's guide with step descriptions and charts, and clogging news.

Access this Web site from http://www.myreportlinks.com

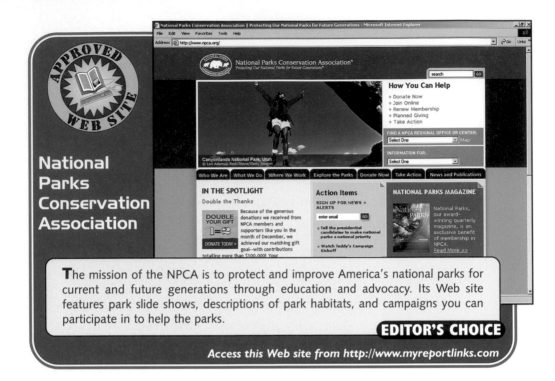

The mission of the NPCA is to protect and improve America's national parks for current and future generations through education and advocacy. Its Web site features park slide shows, descriptions of park habitats, and campaigns you can participate in to help the parks.

EDITOR'S CHOICE

Access this Web site from http://www.myreportlinks.com

Small festivals are a great way to learn more about local culture. One of these is the annual Ramp Festival in Cosby, Tennessee. Ramps are a kind of wild onion. People roam the woods in early May to harvest the bulbs. Ramps are very strong when they are raw, but cooked they are quite a delicacy. People eat them with scrambled eggs or serve them with hoecakes—a kind of corn bread pancake. Washed down with a cup of sassafras tea, it makes a one-of-a-kind, Smoky Mountain meal.

⇥ A NATIONAL TREASURE

Looking out at the view from the observation tower high atop Clingmans Dome, one can see the true splendor of the Smokies. Ridges stretch for miles. Mountains are everywhere. From up high, it looks like a wilderness that has never been touched.

A mere one hundred years ago, the view was a dismal one. Whole tracts of land were bare of trees. Logging roads and railroad tracks scarred the land. Mud washed down the mountains and clogged the streams. The creation of Great Smoky Mountains National Park changed all this. The park is a testimony to the power of nature to take back the land. Even more importantly, it shows what people and their governments can do when they care.

Report Links

The Internet sites described below can be accessed at http://www.myreportlinks.com

▶**Great Smoky Mountains National Park**
Editor's Choice Learn all about Great Smoky Mountains National Park from the official source.

▶**Maps of Great Smoky Mountains National Park**
Editor's Choice Learn the history of the Smokies through maps dating from the sixteenth century.

▶**National Parks Conservation Association**
Editor's Choice Read about how this nonprofit helps to preserve and enhance our national parks.

▶**Horace Kephart: Revealing an Enigma**
Editor's Choice Read about a man whose writings influenced the establishment of the park.

▶**Appalachian Trail Conservancy**
Editor's Choice When visiting the park, you may want to walk part of the Appalachian Trail.

▶**Friends of Great Smoky Mountains National Park**
Editor's Choice Learn how an advocacy group helps Great Smoky Mountains National Park.

▶**Acid Rain Students Site**
Find out what acid rain is, why it is a problem, and what you can do about it.

▶**American Experience: The Rockefellers**
Get to know the Rockefellers, who made free admission to Great Smoky Mountains National Park possible.

▶**Andrew Jackson and the Indian Removal Act**
Find out about President Andrew Jackson's role in moving American Indian tribes out of the Smokies.

▶**Carolina Environmental Diversity Explorations: Elevations and Forest Types**
Explore the range of forest types found in North Carolina's Blue Ridge Mountains.

▶**Cherokee North Carolina**
Get to know the Cherokee Indians, a prominent group in North Carolina.

▶**Discover Bluegrass**
Learn all about the style of music that originated near the Great Smoky Mountains.

▶**Discover Life in America: Great Smoky Mountains National Park All Taxa Biodiversity Inventory**
Learn about a project to determine the biological classification of all plants and animals in the Smokies.

▶*Doubletoe Times*
Check out this site and you'll be able to take part in the clogging craze.

▶**Explore North Carolina**
Learn about the attractions and activities you can experience in North Carolina.

MyReportLinks.com Books

Report Links

The Internet sites described below can be accessed at
http://www.myreportlinks.com

▶**Gatlinburg, Tennessee: Gateway to the Smokies**
Get to know Gatlinburg, Tennessee, and plan a trip there when you visit the Smokies.

▶**Great Smoky Mountains Institute at Tremont**
This nonprofit uses the park as its classroom to connect people and nature.

▶**Hazy Days In Our Parks**
Air pollution is a cause for concern in the Smokies. Learn more about pollution in the parks.

▶**The Joy of Pigs**
Get to know the "misunderstood mammal" that is the pig.

▶**LeConte Lodge**
Find out about the only place to stay in a bed in Great Smoky Mountains National Park.

▶**National Park Foundation**
Learn how volunteers help to promote and maintain America's national parks.

▶**North American Mammals: American Black Bear**
Learn all about the black bear on this Smithsonian Web site.

▶**North American River Otter**
River otters inhabit the Great Smoky Mountains, among other places. Learn all about them here!

▶**Oh, Ranger!: Great Smoky Mountains National Park**
An "At a Glance" view of the park and details about activities to do there are offered on this site.

▶**Salamanders of Tennessee**
You'll be able to tell a variety of salamanders apart after reviewing this Web page.

▶**Sierra Club: Boreal Forest Ecoregion**
Learn about boreal forests, which are found in the high mountaintops of the Smokies.

▶**Temperate Rain Forest**
Find out about the ecology and geography of a temperate rain forest.

▶**Tennessee Vacation**
Explore the state of Tennessee, and plan a vacation trip there.

▶**Welcome to WebRangers**
If you can't make it to a national park to become a Junior Ranger, become a WebRanger instead.

▶**Wildflowers of the Smokies**
Wildflowers contribute to the beauty and biodiversity of the Smokies. See some samples here.

Any comments? Contact us: comments@myreportlinks.com

acid rain—Rain that is polluted with toxins.

adelgid—An aphid-like insect that feeds on trees, often killing the trees in the process.

blight—A disease that spreads rapidly.

bluegrass—Mountain folk music, often played on fiddles, banjos, and guitars.

boreal—Of the north.

canopy—The roof of a forest, formed by the topmost tree branches.

carrion—Dead animals.

clogging—A kind of dance, native to the southern Appalachian Mountains.

Confederacy—States in the South that rebelled against the Union during the American Civil War of 1861–65.

conservation—The act of protecting something so it will exist in the future.

cove–A river valley with very rich soil in the mountains.

DDT—A man-made chemical once used on crops to kill insects.

diversity—Including many different kinds.

elevation—Height measured in distance from sea level.

eminent domain—Government's power to take land or property for the common good.

erosion—The process of eroding, or wearing away by the action of water, wind, or glacial ice.

evergreen—A type of tree that keeps its leaves year round.

extinct—When a type of animal or plant no longer exists in the world.

fungus—A kind of life form, such as mushrooms or molds.

hardscrabble—Making a meager living from poor soil, or marked by poverty.

invasive—Tending to spread or infringe upon.

leach—To leak out from.

livestock—Farm animals, such as pigs and cows.

marsupial—Kind of mammal with a pouch, such as a kangaroo.

mastodon—An extinct relative of the elephant that once lived in North America.

moonshine—Homemade whiskey brewed from corn.

poach—To hunt animals or harvest plants when it is against the law.

ramp—A wild onion that grows in the Smoky Mountains.

sassafras—A tree that settlers used the roots and leaves of to brew tea.

shaman—A priest-like figure who uses magic to heal the sick or to communicate with the spirit world.

sorghum—A plant from which settlers made molasses.

switchback—A zigzag road, trail, or railroad section for climbing steep hills.

toxins—Chemicals that are poisonous to people, animals, or plants.

tropics—A region of the earth near the equator.

understory—A part of the forest, above the forest floor yet under the tree canopy.

Union—The United States of America.

Chapter 1. A Trip to the Great Smoky Mountains

1. George Constanz, *Hollows, Peepers, and Highlanders: An Appalachian Mountain Ecology* (Missoula, Mont.: Mountain Press Publishing Co., 1994), p. 51.

Chapter 2. Cherokee, Mountain Men, and Timber Companies

1. American Park Network, "Geology: Sculpted by Water," *American Park Network: Great Smoky Mountains,* n.d., <http://www.americanparknetwork.com/parkinfo/content.asp?catid=90&contenttypeid=32> (February 10, 2008).

2. National Park Service, "Nature and Science," *National Park Service: Great Smoky Mountains,* n.d., <http://www.nps.gov/grsm/naturescience/index.htm> (February 10, 2008).

3. National Park Service, "Natural Features and Ecosystems," *National Park Service: Great Smoky Mountains,* n.d., <http://www.nps.gov/grsm/naturescience/naturalfeaturesandecosystems.htm> (February 10, 2008).

4. George Wuerthner, *Great Smoky Mountains: A Visitor's Companion* (Mechanicsburg, Pa.: Stackpole Books, 2003), p. 25.

5. John Ehle, *Trail of Tears: The Rise and Fall of the Cherokee Nation* (New York: Doubleday, 1988), p. 1.

6. Michael Read, Loretta Chilcoat, and David Lukas, *Lonely Planet Guide: Great Smoky Mountains and Shenandoah National Parks* (Oakland, Calif.: Lonely Planet Publications, 2005), p. 242.

7. Ehle, p. 19.

8. Golden Ink, "North Georgia Notables: Sequoyah's Talking Leaves," *About North Georgia,* n.d., <http://ngeorgia.com/people/sequoyah.html> (March 9, 2007).

9. Read, Chilcoat, and Lukas, pp. 245–246.

10. Daniel Pierce, *Logging in the Smokies* (Gatlinburg, Tenn.: Great Smoky Mountains Association, 2003), pp. 18–19.

11. Ibid., p. 20.

Chapter 3. The Birth of Great Smoky Mountains National Park

1. George Ellison, in introduction to Horace Kephart, *Our Southern Highlanders* (Knoxville, Tenn.: University of Tennessee Press, 1984), p. xliv.

2. Michael Strutin, *Grist Mills of the Smokies* (Gatlinburg, Tenn.: Great Smoky Mountains Association, 2000), p. 3.

Chapter 4. Plants and Animals of the Smokies

1. John C. Kricher, *Ecology of Eastern Forests* (Boston: Houghton Mifflin, 1988), p. 71.

2. George Constanz, *Hollows, Peepers, and Highlanders: An Appalachian Mountain Ecology* (Missoula, Mont.: Mountain Press Publishing Co.: 1994), p. 32.

3. Michael Read, Loretta Chilcoat, and David Lukas, *Lonely Planet Guide: Great Smoky Mountains and Shenandoah National Parks* (Oakland, Calif.: Lonely Planet Publications, 2005), p. 265.

4. George Wuerthner, *Great Smoky Mountains: A Visitor's Companion* (Mechanicsburg, Pa.: Stackpole Books, 2003), p. 144.

5. Ibid., p. 125.

Chapter 5. The Future of the Great Smoky Mountains

1. George Wuerthner, *Great Smoky Mountains: A Visitor's Companion* (Mechanicsburg, Pa.: Stackpole Books, 2003), p. 78.

2. George Constanz, *Hollows, Peepers, and Highlanders: An Appalachian Mountain Ecology.* (Missoula, Mont.: Mountain Press Publishing Co., 1994), p. 201.

3. Margaret L. Brown. *The Wild East: A Biography of the Great Smoky Mountains* (Gainesville, Fla.: University Press of Florida, 2000), p. 252.

4. Ibid., p. 253.

5. National Park Service, "Non-native Wild Hog Control," *National Park Service, Great Smoky Mountains National Park,* February 2003, <http://www.nps .gov/grsm/parkmgmt/upload/wildhog.pdf> (January 26, 2007).

6. Michael Read, Loretta Chilcoat, and David Lukas, *Lonely Planet Guide: Great Smoky Mountains and Shenandoah National Parks* (Oakland, Calif.: Lonely Planet Publications, 2005), p. 89.

7. National Park Service, "Non-native species," *National Park Service, Great Smoky Mountains National Park,* n.d., <http://www.nps.gov/grsm/naturescience /non-native-species.htm> (January 26, 2007).

8. National Park Service, "Hemlock Woolly Adelgid," *National Park Service, Great Smoky Mountains National Park,* July 2006, <http://www.nps.gov /grsm/naturescience/hemlock-woolly-adelgid .htm> (January 26, 2007).

9. Brown, p. 28.

10. Read, p. 277.

Chapter 6. Things to Do and See in the Smokies

1. Michael Ann Williams, *Great Smoky Mountains Folklife* (Jackson: University Press of Mississippi, 1995), p. 148.

Bauer, Jennifer. *Wildlife, Wildflowers, and Wild Activities: Exploring Southern Appalachia.* Johnson City, Tenn.: Overmountain Press, 2006.

Duncan, Barbara, ed. *The Origin of the Milky Way and Other Living Stories of the Cherokee.* Chapel Hill, N.C.: University of North Carolina Press, 2008.

Feeney, Kathy. *Black Bears (Our Wild World).* Minnetonka, Minn.: NorthWord Press, 2000.

Gove, Dorris. *The Smokies Yukky Book.* Gatlinburg, Tenn.: Great Smoky Mountains Association, 2006.

Houk, Rose. *Great Smoky Mountains National Park: The Range of Life.* Gatlinburg, Tenn.: Great Smokies Association, 2003.

Koontz, Katy, Dick McHugh, and Mitch Moore. *Insiders' Guide to the Great Smoky Mountains,* 5th edition. Guilford, Conn.: Globe Pequot Press, 2007.

Maynard, Charles W. *Going to Great Smoky Mountains National Park.* Helena, Mont.: Farcountry Press, 2008.

Staub, Frank. *America's Mountains.* New York: Mondo Publishing, 2003.

Torres, John Albert. *The Cherokee Trail of Tears and the Forced March of a People.* Enslow Publishers, Inc.: Berkeley Heights, N.J.: MyReportLinks.com Books, 2006.

Wuerthner, George. *Great Smoky Mountains: A Visitor's Companion.* Mechanicsburg, Pa.: Stackpole Books, 2003.